DRIVE IT!

The Complete Book of

RALLYING

**Stuart Turner
& Tony Mason**

Foulis

Haynes

ISBN 0 85429 374 4

First published 1983
Reprinted 1979
Reprinted 1981
Reprinted 1982
Second edition first published November 1983

A FOULIS Motoring Book

Published by
Haynes Publishing Group
Sparkford, Yeovil, Somerset BA22 7JJ

Distributed in USA by:
Haynes Publications Inc.
861 Lawrence Drive, Newbury Park, California 91320 USA

Editor: Rod Grainger
Layout design: Mike King
Dust jacket design: Phill Jennings
Printed and bound by: J. H. Haynes & Co. Ltd.

Previous page: Timo Salonen throws up the dust on the Safari Rally.

Contents

Introduction

If you have picked up this book in a shop because you are mildly curious about rallying but have never actually competed — congratulations! Congratulations because you have stumbled on one of the most exciting and exhilarating sports there is.

Perhaps we'd better start by making it clear exactly what a motor rally is. A motor rally is *not* a race.

A rally involves visiting a number of places within given time limits. Cars usually start at minute intervals and every car in a rally has the same time allowance for each section of the route. Obviously, if every driver in a particular rally did every section within the time limits set then they would all be equal winners, which would be a farce. To guard against this happening, rallies include special stages which are over roads closed to other traffic (such as private farm tracks or Forestry Commission land) and over which cars are timed against the clock.

Some rallies may have just one or two tests to sort out competitors; others like the R.A.C. or Monte Carlo rallies are settled almost entirely on stage results. This means that unless freak weather causes havoc on a rally, the results will normally depend on which is the fastest — or most reliable — car with the best driver.

Almost all European motor manufacturers are involved in rallying in some way or another and they compete for two reasons — development and publicity. A rally driver sweating after the glory (and cash!) of a major rally win will push a car far harder than most development engineers and rallying also makes an ideal testing ground for supporting manufacturers — tyres, lights and brakes are just a few examples.

Although top flight rallying is highly professional, it is still accessible to a private competitor who tackles his rallying in a sensible way. This is one of the attractions of the sport — its heroes are within reach of Mr Average. Anyone taking up rallying for the first time could reasonably expect to be competing in international events without disgracing himself within eighteen months. He would be unlikely to do the same at football or cricket!

We use 'himself' throughout the book for brevity incidentally, but it could just as well be 'herself'. Throughout the history of rallying there have been one or two women quite capable of finishing high up the results tables — in Michèle Mouton's case *very* high up indeed! In fact, with today's constant search for sponsorship to offset rising costs, women drivers possibly have a better chance than men of reaching the upper echelons because of their attractiveness to sponsors.

However, this book isn't really about the upper echelons of rallying, attractive though they may be. Instead it is intended as a basic guide for someone taking up the sport from scratch.

Most amateur golfers have enough of the Walter Mitty in them to dream of winning the Open. Similarly when things are going well and a car is flowing over a special stage, lots of rally drivers must think that, given the breaks, they could be up there scrapping with the best of them. And so they could; if they show enough application and determination. Many of the top drivers around today are within a few years of retirement, so the future looks bright for newcomers. And even if you don't want to become a top line professional rally driver but only do the sport for fun, then you will still get more enjoyment out of your hobby if you go about it in the right way — by getting the right equipment, by studying your driving technique, by preparing your car properly and by tackling the right rallies, in the right order.

In other words, by doing all the things which this book will hopefully teach you.

1 The history

Rally drivers rarely stop to consider the history of their sport, preferring, rightly, to concentrate on preparations for their next event. Nevertheless, rallying has a long and reasonably noble history.

Purists may disagree but really the very first motoring events – such as the Paris to Rouen in 1894 and the Paris-Bordeaux-Paris in 1895 – were rallies, even though they were called races or reliability trials. They were rallies, because in those early days of motoring the *challenge* of actually getting to a place was one of the main incentives, the time taken or the overall position being secondary.

Cars in those events back at the turn of the century carried passengers, just like modern rally cars; they were set off at intervals, just like modern rally cars, and there was a certain amount of navigation or route finding involved, again just as on many modern rallies. The main difference of course was that in those days there was more excitement in motoring; more of a sense of pioneering. Not so today, when at any moment parking seems likely to be made a capital offence!

Although France staged the first motor sport events, we must turn to Germany for the next milestone in any history of rallying because in 1904 Germany saw the Herkomer Trophy, which was a long distance regularity contest for touring cars. Competitors had to maintain strict average speeds between controls, which had to be visited in the right order. Sadly, the regulations were too complex and the rally finished in a flurry of arguments. One thing has thus remained constant throughout the history of rallying – if organisers try to be too clever, competitors will either try to find a way round the regulations or bitch about the results at the finish! All organisers should have a signs on their desks saying "Our job is to provide enjoyment for drivers".

Anyway, getting back to Germany, the Herkomer Trophy faded after a few years but the "Prinz Heinrich Fahrt" took its place. To their everlasting credit, the Imperial Automobile Club persuaded Prince Heinrich of Prussia to put his name to their event – and bear in mind that this was at a time when Germany had just introduced a car tax and speed limits.

The Automobile Club had 130 starters for their first event in 1908, including a couple of fellows not without connections with the motor industry – Bugatti and Opel. After seven days and 14,000 miles the winner was Fritz Erle in a Benz.

The rally spurred the Austrians into organising something similar and their Internationale Alpenfahrt started in 1910. The event grew in stature and by 1914 was attracting entries from all over Europe, including Rolls-Royce. And by this time, incidentally, the name Audi had made an appearance in motor sport – winning the Transalpine Rally in 1913.

While the Germans and Austrians were busy building up their events, further south businessmen in Monte Carlo had watched the increasing popularity of the motor car and considered that an event in January might help fill their hotels at a slack period. So a major milestone in rallying took place with the first Monte Carlo Rally in 1911. The organiser's sensible aim was to get as many people to Monte Carlo as possible and it was much less challenging that the event we know today. Nevertheless some of the elements of today's rally were there, with cars starting from several starting points throughout Europe.

After a disastrous Monte in 1924, when they switched to March, the rally really took hold from 1925 and during the Thirties regularly had over 150 starters. Perhaps January has always been a slow news month for sport – and there are worse places to be in the winter than Monte Carlo – as a result the event has always had wide media attention and even today is perhaps the best known motoring event in Europe, apart from Le Mans.

Perhaps the most important year for British rally enthusiasts was 1929 because that was when the R.A.C. Rally started, although as it was a fairly gentle tour with just a few driving tests, it bore little resemblance to today's glorious thrash through the forests.

Two years later, in 1931, the Royal Motor Union of Liège ran their first Marathon de la Route. The organisers were firm believers in 'no nonsense' rallies with the challenge coming from long and difficult routes, not from nit-picking regulations. In 1951 the event became the Liège-Rome-Liège, then when roads became too crowded over that route, they switched in 1956 to Liège-Sofia-Liège. If you want to see grown men cry, mention "The Liège" to any of the ageing rally stars who once were lucky enough to do it. The sheer challenge of around ninety hours of virtually non-stop motoring over dusty roads in Yugoslavia and Bulgaria was quite something. Occasionally the organisers would be asked by the authorities to put in 'secret checks'. They would solemnly announce this at the drivers' briefing then hold up a card on which, surprise, surprise, was the location of the checks!

The other 'classic' which deserves an honourable mention in any history is the Alpine, or to give it its full title "The Coupe des Alpes". This started in 1949 and through to its demise in the early 1970s provided a tough menu of special sections over mountain passes – so much so that a 'Coupe' for a penalty free run rightly became the most cherished prize in the sport. A 'Gold' Coupe for three Coupes in consecutive years was roughly equivalent to three Olympic Gold Medals.

The late 1950s saw a gradual but positive shift among competitors from amateur to professional (in attitude if not earning power) or if you like, from gentlemen to players. Happily it happened without any interference from promoters. The sport has always been free of squabbles over amateurs and professionals, possibly because it has always been so expensive that even the wealthy competitors have been glad to accept help! We are not suggesting that rally drivers before the Fifties were not serious, obviously they were, but the new breed were virtually full-time professionals earning their living at the sport and therefore able to spend a lot of time practising.

The second big change seen in the late Fifties was the start of the Scandinavian invasion. Eric Carlsson was the pioneering angel and his exploits

Early motor races and reliability trials could really be considered as rallies.

An almost standard Standard on a 1959 Monte Carlo Rally. Roof mounted spotlights are now banned. Note the outside horns!

One of the classic rally cars – the Austin Healey 3000 seen here on Mont Ventoux on the 1962 Alpine Rally.

Leader of the Scandinavian invasion Eric Carlsson comes up to a standing ovation with his Saab after his first R.A.C. Rally win.

The Monte Carlo Rally. Paddy Hopkirk on the way to a win way back in 1964.

The Mini became one of the most popular rally cars in history with successes at every level of the sport. Here is a shot of a typical clubman's Mini-Cooper on the 1965 RAC Rally.

with the Saab became legendary – "The biggest driver in the smallest car" was a journalist's dream.

Rauno Aaltonen was one of the next Scandinavians to make an impact (arriving from a co-driver's seat in the Mercedes team) and then of course they came in hordes.

No-one has really explained why; perhaps the roads in Sweden and Finland give them plenty of opportunity to practise; perhaps the long dark nights do something to the soul which makes good rally drivers. Whatever it is (and if you could bottle it you could make a fortune) you have to accept that, although they are no longer *quite* so dominant, the Scandinavians produce a disproportionate number of rally stars for their population.

If we jump forward ten years to the late Sixties

One of the world's longest rallies – the 1970 London to Mexico won by Hannu Mikkola and Gunnar Palm.

Once thought to be the successor to the big Healeys, the Triumph TR7's rally career was short-lived but relatively successful.

we see the latest change in our history — the growth of sponsorship. Rallying became perhaps more democratic and as youngsters with more ability than cash fought to reach the top, they naturally turned to sponsors to lubricate their efforts. People like Castrol and Shell and others had long supported people in racing and rallying but they suddenly realised that they would get better value if more people were aware of their involvement — hence the sponsors' decal (or sticker). Later, cars appeared in properly planned total colour schemes.

With the advent of sponsors — particularly those from non-motoring areas who brought in fresh ideas — came professional public relations and with them better media coverage. Rallying still doesn't receive proper media attention, either on television or in the national press, though what there is gets increasingly international with Swedish TV covering the Safari, German TV covering the R.A.C. Rally and so on. All good stuff for manufacturers and sponsors.

Other historical milestones? The growth of stage events at the expense of road rallies in Britain — inevitable with crowded roads and faster cars, but still sad. Apart from anything else road rallies provide a great training ground and they have even attracted members of the Royal Family as competitors which does the sport no harm at all.

Safety in cars has improved, which has to be a very good thing; the increasing popularity of rallying has produced safety problems with spectators, which is obviously *not* a good thing. Then the late Seventies saw the re-birth of one-make championships designed to keep costs down — also a good thing because it means that team managers looking for talent can study the results knowing that Fred is quick because he is a better driver, not because he has spent more on his car than Albert.

In summary, therefore, most of the changes throughout the history of rallying have been gradual and sensible. Go forth young man knowing your sport has a good pedigree!

2 Types of rallies

Although no two rallies are alike it is possible to place them in certain categories; at one end of the scale the small club social rally and at the other the glamorous, rugged full-blown International. Each type has its own specialists, its own fans and its own champions. The various types require different skills from competitors and perhaps the only constant factor is that a *reliable* car of some sort is needed for success – speed and performance being less critical on many events.

You will need a car, driver and a co-driver/navigator/passenger for any rally but it is impossible to generalise on the role of the person occupying the passenger seat; certainly it is difficult to adjudicate on the ratio of importance between driver and navigator. On a club rally where there are numerous navigational problems, the responsibility for success falls fairly and squarely on the navigator; as long as the driver can operate the controls of the car there is no reason why he should not chauffeur his able colleague to victory.

It is also possible for an unbalanced crew to win another type of rally altogether – a good special stage driver can frequently win a very simple stage rally even if accompanied by a very simple co-driver. There has even been facetious talk of co-drivers being replaced by sacks of potatoes on easier stage rallies!

However these are the extremes and the basic recipe for success in rallying is a good combination of crew talents plus a reliable vehicle, one prepared with care and attention to detail.

Let's now look at the different types of event, starting in the lower echelons and working up to the world-famous rallies. We hope devotees of the car treasure hunt will forgive us if we start with their particular event which is often regarded as the lowest end of the scale.

Whenever social groups gather, a car treasure hunt is likely to find itself on their social calendar. Most countries have regulations controlling the running of events on public highways and Britain is no exception. It is against the law to run on the public highway any unauthorised motoring event of more than twelve cars wherein the driver may receive any form of time penalty. Therefore, organisers of treasure hunts can break the law unless they take care. Nevertheless it is still possible to organise successful treasure hunts which stay well within the law, yet provide innocent entertainment for the participants.

Treasure hunts tend to take place in daylight hours and the basic requirement is to solve clues or gather pieces of information as the car travels round a gentle route. The route itself may be given by clues and questions; some organisers lay on a mobile *Times* crossword, others prefer a more light-hearted approach.

Treasure hunts have sometimes caused problems with reports of disturbances in sleepy villages, ranging from the desecration of churchyards to the interruption of retired Colonels' Sunday afternoon naps, but *if* (and *only* if) the treasure hunts are organised with care they can be good fun and can even be regarded as good navigator training. They certainly provide mental exercise.

Despite the social nature of the treasure hunt, prospective organisers would do well to advise the police of the passage of the event and might find the event more acceptable if the crews are not required to leave the cars too often. Great care should, of course, be taken with the use of narrow lanes in the route.

The only rallies which do not require full authorisation from the Royal Automobile Club Motor Sports Association Ltd (who act on behalf of the Department of the Environment) are those in which twelve cars or less compete. Even so, these

Oops! Nearly a wrong slot for Peter Gerbez' and Gareth Jones' Escort on a Cheshire road event.

events are subject to some restrictions and organisers must advise the police and the R.A.C. of any event that is planned.

The organisation of a twelve car rally is obviously much easier than a bigger one, and such events are popular with motor clubs who frequently run them as training events for less experienced members. As they are usually run to the rigid rules of the bigger events, they make a good starting point for the raw beginner. They are often short in distance and will probably take place during an evening. Like most road events, it is advisable to run them during darkness as the narrow lanes of Britain are less than ideal for safe competition motoring in daylight hours.

Moving on from twelve car events, the 'closed-to-club' rally is next on the agenda. This event will be organised to conform to all the rules and regulations applying to any major road rally; the route will have to be authorised in detail but participation in the event will be restricted to members of the promoting club only. The mileage will probably not be very great but neither will the expense of competing (nor the awards for that matter!). It is not necessary to have an R.A.C. competition licence in

order to compete in a 'closed-to-club' rally; all you need is a Club membership card. The next stage up is the closed co-promoted event, confined to members of not more than six clubs.

Whatever the particular levels, there are two basic types of rally in Britain. One is the road rally where the car and crew are required to pass given points at specified times and spend the entire period of the rally on public roads. Naturally a restriction on the maximum required average speed is imposed to avoid racing on the public highway or exceeding statutory speed limits.

The other type of event is the special stage rally where cars enjoy relatively easy public road sections but are required to cover stages on private land at high speeds. It is very much a 'Jekyll and Hyde' operation as drivers have to cope with gentle road sections then fierce and fast stages. The stages can be found on private farm tracks, disused airfields and railway lines or in the magnificent forest tracks of Britain. Enterprising organisers have been known to use private roads in stately homes, factories, the roads around sewerage plants, and believe it or not, the subterranean tracks of a coal-mine. The last named was featured on a Swedish rally many moons ago, but then there are no bounds to the imagination of rally organisers in Sweden and Finland. Scandinavian rally stages frequently traverse frozen lakes and rivers, sometimes with the stage carved out of the snow on a lake's frozen surface by a snow plough a few hours before the cars are due.

British stages can be muddy, rocky and rough, but are very popular with competitors even in spite of the higher costs of competing on a stage rally rather than a road event.

Moving up the scale, probably the most popular grade of rally is the 'Restricted' club rally. Here a club will extend an invitation to other neighbouring or prominent motor clubs (usually up to a maximum of sixteen) whose members will be entitled to compete in the event upon production of a current club membership card plus the competition licence of the appropriate grade.

Stage and road rallies are both popular at Restricted grade and usually last one full day (in the case of stage events) or one full night (in the case of both) rather than the half day or half night of lesser events.

As Restricted rallies are run to R.A.C. regula-

tions it is necessary for competing cars to conform to all the requirements laid down by the R.A.C., so they will have to pass the inspection of a Scrutineer before the event starts. Stage and road events have different requirements but all relate to safety, be it the safety of competitors or that of spectators.

Noise level is an important factor in the case of all road rallies and cars are scrutineered before the start of any event. Should an exhaust system be damaged or develop a fault during an event, the crew will probably find themselves penalised or excluded by noise marshals who lurk in the lanes.

Road rallies up to Restricted level may have the routes defined by map references or more intricate methods. Either way, the navigator will play an important role. On a really difficult navigational event the person in the passenger seat plays by far the more important part. Most of the route will confine itself to lanes and byways, some non-surfaced and occasionally non-charted. Some sections, on the more deserted parts of the route, may be timed to the second but there are restrictions on the number of 'selective' sections allowed. 'Selectives', by the way, should only be run after midnight. Maps will be of great importance and

Bill Gwynne drives a Mk.III Escort on a 'Cambrian News' road rally.

Make sure your car is waterproofed – there are often deep fords on road rallies. Welshmen Huw Jenkins and Kevin Thomas are seen in a TR7 on the Rali Mynydd Du.

It's possible to use a standard, unsponsored, 'road car' on stages. This Escort RS is driven by Roger Collinson and Stephen Bye on a smooth but wet Northern forest event.

A typical Manx International Rally stage demonstrated by Jimmy McRae's and Ian Grindrod's Opel Ascona 400.

almost certainly the excellent Ordnance Survey maps will be used.

Numerous road rally Championships exist, won by performance on selected events which qualify; in some championships competitors have to register to qualify, in others they score automatically if they finish in a scoring position. There are area championships, inter-club championships and even national championships devoted to road rallies. By far the best known is the Motoring News Rally Championship which has run without a break since 1960 while the B.T.R.D.A. Silver Star Championship has run from even earlier than that — see what we meant by the sport having a noble history?

Incidentally one area of training for navigators which, for some reason, is rarely mentioned in motoring circles is the sport of orienteering. Orienteers are required to visit various points on a map — on foot by the way — covering different types of terrain, reaching the finish within a specified time. Motor rallying and orienteering both have a fanatical following in Scandinavia and the whole question of map reading, course plotting and "reading the countryside" is common to both. The only difference is that the orienteering map reader does not need a car or driver (many navigators interpret this as a distinct advantage!) No one would seriously describe orienteering as a type of car rally but as a navigational training exercise it is worth more than

a passing thought. Many drivers are far from physically fit — maybe they, too, could benefit from a spot of orienteering!

Although road rallies in Britain will not be found at any level higher than Restricted grade, it is worth mentioning that some European events attract British road rally addicts. There are numerous small tarmac events, particularly in Belgium, of at least one night's duration which present good values as they are inexpensive by international standards. Further incentives are often given by the organisers who arrange free entries, cheap hotel accommodation and even low cost ferry fares.

Stage rallies operate at all grades in Britain, the Restricted grade being by far the most common. Many of these rallies have access to the wide variety of loose surface tracks in Britain's forests, although the Forestry Commission has stringent rules about the amount of use each road may have, as well as on the charges to be levied on organisers and routes to be taken. However without the use of these tracks the British rally scene would be a lot poorer and have far less capable drivers in its ranks.

The level of crew responsibility changes in the case of stage rallies, the driver assuming a far more important role. The car must be tough and well prepared, and will need greater performance than its road rally counterpart. Tyre patterns become more

17

Finland's Rally of 1000 Lakes is famous for its 'yumps' here demonstrated by a Mitsubishi Lancer 2000.

A typical African rally scene for Per Eklund and Ragnar Spjuth in their Toyota Celica on the Rallye Cote d'Ivoire.

An interesting pavé road surface for Jimmy McRae's Opel Ascona on the island of Madeira.

Britain's Terry Kaby with Mike Nicholson going well on Lombard-RAC Rally in a Vauxhall Chevette HSR.

Markku Alén's Lancia looks purposeful at the scrutineering bay of the Lombard-RAC Rally.

important and conversation turns to differentials, cams, special driveshafts, five-speed gearboxes and the like.

Total stage mileage can range from 25 to a hundred miles or more and the road mileage can be literally anything; it will probably consist of main road or even motorway driving at times, all totally non-competitive. Single venue events are also popular; here the competing cars attempt several stages within a large park, quarry or disused airfield and run to full rally regulations but never venture onto the public road which, of course, makes the organisers' lot a little easier. The same stage may often be used twice or more.

On a stage rally the pressure is really on the driver to drive as quickly as possible from the start of each stage to the finish. The length of the stages varies from a mere mile or two to twenty miles or more, although anything above twenty is rare. Organisers usually place prominent arrows at junctions and bends, and mark hazard spots on the track and in the road book; start and finish points are clearly marked by large boards, too. The navigator, who is starting to assume the role of co-driver (we shall discuss the delicate terminology later) has to keep an eye on the whole proceedings, though he won't have to find the route from the map (although some co-drivers on British events previously found that following marked maps of forests helped their

driver considerably – which led to their use being banned on many events!). However, the co-driver will keep an eye on the stage and help confirm arrows to his driver. He will tell him how far it is to the finish in the event of a puncture or other problem so that the driver can decide whether to stop or limp on, and he will check the time carefully on arrival at the finish of a stage. There are stage target times, times of arrival and departure at stages, fuel halts, road controls, etc., to think about so the co-driver is kept fully occupied.

National special stage rallies have a minimum stage total of sixty miles and are open to any national competition licence holder. They tend to concentrate on forestry roads and consist entirely of special stages. These full day or full night events usually attract a good entry of well-prepared cars, all of which conform to the regulations stipulated for a national event. The rallies take place in all parts of the United Kingdom and usually qualify for a major championship.

There are a number of British International *forest* rallies – other than the famed Lombard R.A.C. – and it is the aim of many Clubmen to compete in one of these events during their rally careers. Using the best of the forest tracks available to them, these rallies enjoy a high standard of organisation, and often attract the top overseas drivers, so giving Britons the taste of International rally conditions.

Quattro in America. John Buffum throws up the dust in the Pike National Forest to win the Miller Centennial Rally, and enhance his reputation as top American Rally Driver.

The Welsh and Scottish Rallies are by far the best known of these: British works and dealer teams and overseas works teams enter these events, giving them a reasonably International flavour.

The pinnacle in Britain is of course the Lombard R.A.C. Since its move to the forests in 1961 the R.A.C. has gone from strength to strength and now enjoys the healthiest entry list of any rally in the world. All the top drivers rate it as one of their favourite events and the unpractised forests certainly put all the drivers on an even footing. It has become firmly established as a major spectator and sporting event in Britain and over two million people turn out to watch the five-day rally each year; millions more follow it on TV and radio.

Before leaving the British scene, mention must be made of the very popular and extremely demanding tarmac rallies. Thanks to the favourable views of their governments to closing public roads, Ireland and the Isle of Man provide opportunities for British drivers to gain the sort of experience once only available to Continentals. Ireland boasts the Easter weekend Circuit of Ireland, as well as the Donegal, Galway and other rallies and the Isle of Man produces the Manx International and the shorter Manx Stages each year. The events are pure stage rallies and most cars run on racing tyres and even lowered suspension. Events last three or four days; and thanks to the high speeds and unforgiving bumps, often have fewer finishers than any forest rally of comparable length. A small stage rally in the holiday Channel Island of Jersey is now in the British calendar too.

Mainland Europe still plays host to the World Rally Circus for much of the rally year; there are numerous major events held in the classic mountains of Europe, and very demanding they are too. Some British Club drivers make sorties to compete in these European events, particularly the small International rallies in Spain, Portugal or

Andrew Cowan winning the 1977 London to Sydney Rally in a Mercedes-Benz – nine years after he won the first in a Hillman Hunter.

Southern France, as these can be combined with a holiday.

The world of rallying has spread its wings and there are major events in every corner of the world. Large countries with sparse populations permit long, fast open road sections, and on African rallies cars can go for hours without ever touching an asphalt road.

Developing countries are keen to add rallying to their list of attractions and the African and Middle Eastern countries are now employing the talents of British rally organisers to get them on their feet.

Rallying is also becoming a popular sport in America and that country appears to be moving well away from the 'navigational nightmares' of the Seventies. Events are held in most States and the better events, like the Reno and Frontier Nevada rallies attract a good quality international entry, calling for fast driving on the superb dirt roads which are available to the organisers. The Sports Car Club of America runs an important national championship and has been known to feature events with such quaint titles as 'Big Bend Bash', 'Happiness is Sunrise' and 'Press on Regardless'! One driver in particular, John Buffum, has been by far the fastest and most successful driver in the domestic championships for many years, but he has also made regular trips across the Atlantic where he

One of the top road rally crews of the eighties, Mike Hutchinson and Nigel Harris on their way to another win on a Welsh road event. Note the use of intercom sets as described in Chapter 8. Note also the Institute of Advanced Motorists' badge!

has competed on equal terms with top European drivers. Buffum has taken back many ideas to help American rallying to develop.

There are also numerous rallies in the Eastern bloc countries and the U.S.S.R. sends its State Rally Team on periodic sorties outside the Soviet Union. With cars noted for their ruggedness rather than for out-and-out speed, the determined Moskvitch and Lada drivers have frequently scooped team awards from under the noses of their faster rivals on events including the 1000 Lakes in Finland and even the Lombard R.A.C.

Rallying is popular in the Far East too, with many big prize money events which attract visiting drivers. Thailand, the Philippines, and even Hong Kong have hosted such rallies, while the Japanese domestic rally calendar is very full, with events of all types — particularly those of a navigational nature.

Australia is noted for its rugged style of events and New Zealand has a strong rallying fraternity, having hosted a World Championship round on a number of occasions. So too have Brazil and Argentina, while most other South American countries promote long, tough events of their own.

So, regardless of politics, petrol prices, creed or colour, there are rallies in every corner of the world. There are rallies on tiny islands in the Southern hemisphere, there are rallies hundreds of miles north of the Arctic circle, and, if that is not enough, there are trans-Sahara events and even occasional trans-world marathons.

3 How and where to start

The simplest way to get the flavour of rallying is as a spectator. If you take this route, do remember that spectators cause more complaints from the public than rally competitors, so

DO — drive sensibly
— obey marshals' instructions
— park where directed
— arrive at stages early and be prepared for long walks into the forests
— watch out for flying stones (a rally car at speed can hurl them like bullets)
— keep well back from the rally road

DON'T — leave litter
— drive like a maniac on public roads
— stand in silly places
— smoke in forest areas or where a car is being serviced
— take a dog with you

If spectating whets your appetite then the next level of involvement is marshalling. This takes you closer to the action and organisers will welcome your services with open arms, BUT, marshalling brings with it responsibilities — above all you must be reliable and responsible and you must follow the organisers' instructions. Don't be officious — rallying should be fun for all concerned.

If having marshalled, you want to take up rallying as a competitor, the first thing to do is to join a motor club which is recognised by the R.A.C. To obtain recognition a club has to be reasonably well established and must operate in accordance with rules drawn up by the R.A.C. There are over eight hundred recognised clubs in Britain and apart from providing a starting point for budding drivers and navigators they also offer a good social side.

The R.A.C. Motor Sports Association Ltd, 31 Belgrave Square, London SW1X 8QH (Telephone 01-235-8601) will be able to supply a list of clubs in your area or, better still, you should buy a copy of their Year Book which includes addresses of *all* motor clubs as well as a lot of other useful information.

Most clubs have a leaning towards one particular branch of the sport so if there are several in your area write to the secretaries to find out their main interests — as a budding rally driver it would make no sense to join a club specialising in hillclimbing.

Later in your rally career you will almost certainly join more than one club, including one of the better rally clubs so that you get invitations to the best rallies.

There are a handful of *national* clubs like the British Trial and Rally Drivers Association but most clubs are based in one particular locality and are linked with other clubs in their area to form Regional Associations of the R.A.C.

It is pretty certain that you will find a motor club based in your nearest town, so join it.

Each year the average motor club organises, or co-organises with neighbouring clubs, a handful of road and stage rallies of a "Closed-to-club" status and possibly one major Restricted rally as well; in addition it probably organises some twelve-car rallies. It will almost certainly hold regular club meetings, film shows and social functions.

It is obviously wise to decide at an early stage if you wish to concentrate on driving or navigating, although a dabble at both is an excellent thing before you get too serious. At this early stage, the potential driver need not have the latest specification of rally car. In fact, it's a positive *disadvantage* to possess such a vehicle for it could be dangerous if the capability of the car is way ahead of his skills. Better to start with a modest vehicle and work up to faster machinery.

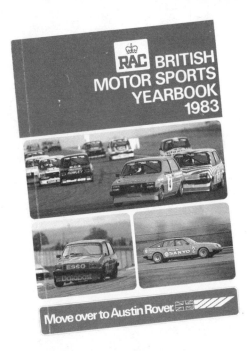

RAC BRITISH MOTOR SPORTS YEARBOOK 1983

Move over to Austin Rover.

Essential reading – the RAC MSA 'blue book' which covers all the rules, regulations and fixtures for British Motorsport.

The legendary Roger Clark started rallying in a Ford 5 cwt van while Russell Brookes borrowed an Austin Westminster before he graduated to a Morris Minor 1000 of his own. Hannu Mikkola started on the road to super-stardom on local events in a secondhand Volvo PV 544. There are other stars, who used to borrow their company car for innocent events but we would not recommend this to anyone who hopes to get a gold watch for long service with their company!

The point we are making is that *any* type of car will be acceptable at these early stages and whatever the performance of the car you will soon see if you, as a driver or navigator, have any intention or any desire to progress to greater things.

A driver should simply see that the car is mechanically sound, has good underbody protection, good lights and tyres and, of course, good brakes. Obviously an experienced navigator can be an enormous help to a driver but it must be made quite clear that the driver is hoping to *learn* from his early events; he should not try to impress the experienced partner with great heroics.

The navigator's beginning will be very similar to the driver's although *his* major investment will be a few pencils, one or two simple navigational instruments and an Ordnance Survey map or two. The problem of pairing is very much the same as the driver's – don't select a very experienced driver (if he'll have you) as you'll be so frightened of making a mistake that you will probably make one within a mile of the start.

Be completely honest with your partner and preferably learn together.

Many successful navigators started rallying at tender ages, among them are Arne Hertz, Fred Gallagher and Ian Grindrod. Mike Broad, who navigated the winning car on the last London-Sydney rally, competed in his first event at fourteen., Some navigators start before they can drive a car and many do not even possess a car – we mention this because some people think that they cannot join a car club if they do not own a car. Not so! A navigator is fortunate because it will not cost a lot of money to practise.

Grasp every opportunity to compete on a rally, no matter how small. Practise map reference plotting and practise more difficult navigational exercises too. Get hold of old route cards from previous rallies and go through them.

Some navigators have been known to sit in a darkened room in a rocking chair holding a torch, plotting map referencs under simulated rally car conditions. It's not a bad idea! If you can persuade a friend to take you for short drives, do so, and read the map while you go. You can follow a prescribed route from an old route card or even a route you have devised yourself. Try a few 'table top rallies' – motor clubs often run these as social evenings. Above all, gain every bit of experience you can – practise, practise, practise. Some top co-drivers have even been known to take Ordnance Survey maps to bed with them to practise plotting there! More normal beings might have other bedroom activities in mind, of course.

While budding navigators are gaining as much map experience as possible, the driver should be concentrating on building up experience in the driving seat. Drive on as many events as you can. Don't worry if your car is unsuitable for the event in question, don't worry if you cannot win – just keep piling up those vital hours of experience. Loose surface auto-tests are always good and several clubs organise events of this nature. You may say that dodging plastic pylons is not what you aim to do for the rest of your motor sport career – don't worry, just think of the pylon as a fir tree or gatepost. There'll come a time when you'll be glad of that pylon dodging practice.

Many top drivers have spent time gaining racing experience in their early careers while Stig Blomqvist and Per Eklund found rallycross good training for developing judgement, timing and car control.

Practise driving under all conditions. Don't go berserk racing around the lanes but do go for long drives on deserted tracks in adverse weather conditions. And if there is snow or fog – get out and practise. You'll be surprised how these two elements can alter rally results. Finnish drivers Markku Alén and Henri Toivonen frequently practised fog driving early in their careers.

Many top drivers started driving at a very early age; some of those brought up in a motoring environment were capable drivers by the time they were ten years old! Needless to say, they only practised on private tracks or in fields. Conversely, twice British Champion Jimmy McRae didn't compete in a rally until he was nearly 30!

Whatever your age or background the message is clear; drive, drive, drive! Please do not trespass when practising your driving. **Do not,** ever, try to get onto Forestry Commission land or *any* private land; this will not only spoil your training plans if you are caught but, much more important, it will have a damaging effect on rally relations with land owners.

Remember that a good rally driver needs a combination of talents. He should have good balance, extremely good judgement, good reactions and good timing. The Americans have an apt saying to describe the cause of many motor sport accidents. "It was the right foot in the wrong place".

Speaking of balance, you may find motor cycle experience helpful. Tony Pond, Pentti Airikkala and Jimmy McRae swear that it was trail riding that helped them hone their driving skill. World Champion Walter Rohrl was West German downhill ski champion and attributes his car control to that.

All the top rally crews are strong believers in personal fitness and most of them are strictly teetotal and non-smokers; Henri Toivonen even keeps strictly to a specially designed diet prepared by a dietician.

Although it is useful to try rallies with different partners, there is no doubt that you are likely to have more success if you develop a permanent partnership. It is important to develop a rapport with your partner particularly if you intend to compete in road rallies because the best road rally crews will almost be able to read each other's minds. A driver will understand instructions merely by the intonation in the navigator's voice when giving an instruction. Similarly, a navigator will be able to forestall a driver's question about the distance to petrol, or the penalty marks to date. A driver must be kept supplied with appropriate information (not too many trivia) although they do have an annoying habit of asking for it at the most inconvenient moments.

Even in stage rallies a good partnership is an advantage and when one starts to use pace notes the degree of trust and rapport which exists between the crew can be vital.

One of the problems encountered by the navigator in the early stages of map reading may be the dreaded travel sickness. Don't be put off by this rather unpleasant problem. Remember that most of today's top co-drivers have been sick at some time or other and travel sickness is usually overcome by confidence: confidence in your driver, confidence in your ability and confidence in your stomach. However, it will be wise to take one or two precautions at an early stage. Although some of the more experienced co-drivers eat copious supplies of fat-

tening, filling food before an event (they work on the principle that they never know when it might be their last meal) it is wise to eat sensible amounts of *non-greasy* food before a rally. Naturally it would be irresponsible for either crew member to consider taking any alcohol. Don't starve yourself completely – you will not work accurately or efficiently if you are suffering from hunger pangs.

One of the major causes of travel sickness is the constant change in length of vision for the navigator – from the map to the road ahead and vice-versa. To avoid this, try to keep the knees which support the map-board as high as possible so that your eyes do not have to glance too far up and down when reading the map or when looking out of the windscreen – probably 50% of your time will be devoted to each. The other precaution is to have full harness seat belts **fastened as tightly as possible.** This keeps you at one with the car and although you might feel as though you are being shaken to pieces, you will find less of a sickness problem.

Ian Grindrod suffered badly from sickness when he first started rallying (as a child he had been unable to travel for two miles on a bus without the inevitable happening) and he regarded the travel sickness problems as the greatest mental barrier to be overcome. He claims that confidence in one's own ability lessens the problem by fifty percent and after he had won his first small award he was never sick again!

Another tip from the top co-drivers is to practise reading anything you can lay your hands on when travelling in a car. You might be accused of being anti-social if you sit with your nose buried in a book when riding as a passenger in a car but it *can* help your problem.

If you really have a sickness problem and don't seem able to cure it, see your doctor, but make sure you tell him about your navigational role as some of the stronger travel drugs (only available on prescription) have a very strong drowsiness effect.

Both crew members should read as much about rallying as they can (there are lots of starving rally writers about – they all need your help). Go to the rally film shows, listen and ask questions when your local club has an expert competitor as a guest speaker. Go to forums to listen and ask – you'll be surprised what you can learn. Even a fellow panellist learnt a new car control trick after listening to one of Hannu Mikkola's answers on a rally forum some years ago.

In this age of high video technology and sophisticated show business techniques, the beginner has many opportunities to see and hear a great deal about rallying and to meet top crews as the sport's major sponsors put on rally shows for the clubs. Never miss one!

A driver can also learn useful technical tips from these shows and from lectures, forums and

Autotests can provide very useful experience in car control. Trevor Smith proves the point well – he was National Autotest Champion then took up rallying and became BTRDA Rally Champion, too.

discussions, and he should certainly be reading as much as he can about rally preparation. Although some drivers are not particularly mechanically-minded, it is an advantage for the driver to have some mechanical knowledge.

A navigator usually has no interest whatsoever in the mechanics of a car, but it is again not a bad thing to have some basic knowledge. However your career develops and however many service crews you will employ, you'll still need to do your own running repairs from time to time.

Talking of service, you'll probably decide to take a service crew along when you do stage events (though only, repeat only, if permitted by the regulations). This may well be necessary if only to change wheels if you're lucky enough to have a choice of tyres. The service crew can fall into two categories – either a 'well equipped friend' (we're not talking about large ladies) or an estate car or van full of parts and tools. Either way, someone is going to have to pay.

Some club members will be delighted to act as a service crew and pay their own petrol or hotel costs as it is their way of enjoying the sport – others may need a contribution. One thing is certain, you'll need to work out costs in detail and be very clear about who pays what long before the event. Good rally friendships have been ruined by financial mis-understandings.

While on the topic of money we should also explain that there is no hard and fast rule for sharing expenses. Rallying is an expensive pastime, although the amount you spend depends on your level of participation. Basically, drivers are usually responsible for all the costs of car preparation, including parts, although it really depends on the personal financial situation of the competitors. It is not uncommon to share entry fees and running costs between navigator and driver, but on a stage event where the driver gains the greater kudos this may not be acceptable.

Whatever you decide, make sure it is cut and dried *before* you set off and also make sure who gets the prize money if any comes your way. However, as this chapter is about the beginner in motor sport, it is unlikely you'll see much prize money at this stage.

It is necessary for the driver to be **absolutely**

sure his car is properly insured for any event and while on the subject of insurance we should mention life insurance. Many policies exclude dangerous sports and for insurance purposes a rally is considered a dangerous sport. Some insurance companies can include an endorsement which allows rallying to take place, so make sure that yours is one – if not, change; an insurance broker will probably give you the best advice. Although we do not wish to become too macabre, a brief word about wills might not go amiss. As the events you enter grow in size, so will the distances you travel and there are, regrettably, occasional deaths involving travel and motor sports. See your solicitor to make sure your affairs are in order.

4 Personal equipment

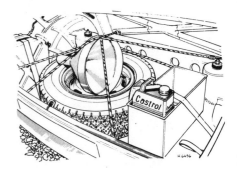

Safety and comfort are the two things to consider when choosing the first category of personal equipment – clothing.

Top crews pay close attention to both matters and very expensive flame-resistant overalls, gloves, underwear and socks are the order of the day for them. If you are lucky enough to find yourself in this category you will be fully *au fait* with the latest, safest rally wear and more than likely your sponsor or team will pay for most of it! However, for lesser mortals the choice of clothing is still important.

Competitors on smaller road rallies will probably not need to go to the expense of purchasing overalls, but may simply wear jeans and pullover. Some drivers prefer 'shirt-sleeve order', others drive in a rally jacket with the car window open. Incidentally, drivers' window-opening habits should be borne in mind when navigators are planning *their* rallying wardrobe.

Footwear and gloves are again a matter of personal choice, but drivers' shoes should have no projections which might foul the pedals. Gloves should have chamois leather backs if you are likely to use them to clean the screen. Remember that whatever you wear, you're likely to find yourself scrambling under the car at some point so it's advisable not to wear your best suit.

A navigator on a road event may prefer to wear a jacket, or something with a few pockets, as a well organised individual will carry erasers, spare pencils and other paraphernalia. He may also collect route-check cards and other bits of paper *en route.* Again, the latest Gucci footwear is not recommended for the navigator as he will probably find himself running along a ditch to a control at some time during a rally. Waterproof shoes are worth considering – in Canadian and Scandinavian winter rallies many co-drivers wear fur-lined boots with studded soles.

Rally overalls are, of course, widely worn by drivers and navigators and they certainly make sense. Being purpose-built they save other clothing, keep the body at the right temperature, and may even make the crew feel and perform better. Fireproof overalls, whilst seldom compulsory in rallying, are popular. They are an undoubted safety precaution, although they can be a trifle uncomfortable on hot long-distance events.

Colour and design of overalls are matters of personal choice, although light colours are safer; you may find yourself dancing around in a forest track, or changing a wheel, when another competitor comes along and you'll be seen more easily. Some overall manufacturers will only contemplate manufacturing one-piece suits. These are safer if the driver has to be pulled out of a car by outside helpers, although two-piece overalls seem more popular with rally crews.

Decorate your overalls with badges by all means, but try to keep a sense of neatness and decorum. Appearances are important and help the sport, so keep unnecessary and vulgar signs off your clothing. It's worth remembering that your most important decal (probably your sponsor's) should be as close to the chin as possible as this is the one seen on photographs and film and television interviews. Some people embroider their blood group on their overalls; a sensible safety precaution but professional crews will also have this on a wrist bracelet or on a disc round their neck as, in the unhappy event of an accident, their overalls might not reach hospital with them.

Rally jackets come in a proliferation of sizes, colours and designs and if you are not lucky enough to be given one by your team or sponsor then choose a practical one. As good a rule as any is to choose the type the works drivers wear. They are likely to be the right weight, be comfortable to wear and have pockets of the right size. Certainly the co-driver's jacket should have pockets large enough to carry passports, licences and rally documents like time cards (the latter may have to be stored safely during waits at main rest halts or controls). Make sure the rally jacket has a built-in hood; many have fold away hoods and these are particularly suitable because there will be a cold, wet and windy night when you will welcome something to keep your head warm whilst waiting at a control or stage start (or when waiting for a breakdown truck!). Modern motoring fashions seem to have abandoned the time-honoured bobble-hat but you'll find that a cap or hat of some sort is useful if you need to leave the car in bad weather.

Talking of headgear brings us on to safety helmets — an essential part of rally equipment on all but the smallest road rally. When selecting a crash helmet make sure you choose one that fits you properly. **A badly fitting crash helmet can be more dangerous than no helmet at all.** In any case, unless you feel comfortable you will not be able to function in the rally properly. As a guide the following may be useful:

Buy the best helmet you can afford, and the best seatbelts. Here Henri Toivenen shows his full-face helmet with intercom fitted integrally.

Crash helmet size chart

Size in inches (by tape measure)	$20\frac{1}{2}$	$20\frac{7}{8}$	$21\frac{1}{4}$	$21\frac{5}{8}$	22	$22\frac{1}{2}$	$22\frac{7}{8}$	$23\frac{1}{4}$	$23\frac{5}{8}$	24	$24\frac{3}{8}$
Hat size	$6\frac{3}{8}$	$6\frac{1}{2}$	$6\frac{5}{8}$	$6\frac{3}{4}$	$6\frac{7}{8}$	7	$7\frac{1}{8}$	$7\frac{1}{4}$	$7\frac{3}{8}$	$7\frac{1}{2}$	$7\frac{5}{8}$
Helmet size	Extra Small	Extra Small	S	S	M	M	L	L	Extra Large	Extra Large	Extra Large

Sizes in different makes may vary. Make sure the helmet you select is not too tight and certainly not too slack. A driver on one Manx Rally found that everything had gone dark after one particularly ferocious hump; his helmet was far too big and had slipped over his eyes. Not the safest way to go rallying!

Helmets are expensive but remember you are protecting a vital part of your body.

Decide whether you wish to wear a full-face or open-face model. There's a price difference and some people find a slightly claustrophobic effect when wearing a full face, but they are safe and find an increasing use in rallying today. In some countries it is compulsory for both members of crew to wear full-face helmets. One word of caution, if you wear a fully enclosed helmet, make sure you can get an adequate supply of fresh air, otherwise you may perform below par simply through breathing stale air.

Whatever style or make of helmet you wear, make sure that your choice carries the latest British Standard numbers and other acceptable national markings, thereby making it conform with R.A.C. regulations. The number of types and makes of helmet that are now fully approved is considerable and any list would quickly be out of date, but the following list shows acceptable standard marks at the time of publication:

1	AFNOR Competition	(France)	S.72.302 & S.72.303
2	British Standard Institute		BS 2495 77 & BS 2495 77 AMT 5
3	DIN 4848 ONS –	(Germany)	OMK/ONS
	DS ⎰Combined ⎱	(Denmark)	2124.1
4	SFS ⎱"NORDIC"⎰	(Finland)	3653
	SIS ⎰Standard ⎱	(Sweden)	88.24.32
5	SNELL	(U.S.A.)	1975 & 1980

One half of an intercom set.

The R.A.C. Motor Sports Association now recognise all the above standards. Helmets are – or should be – checked by the scrutineer before most major rallies and it is important that yours carries the approval number. Stickers to indicate that they are of an approved type have to be carried on helmets and R.A.C. scrutineers will issue the latest labels with serialised numbering.

The R.A.C. Motor Sports Association operates a security labelling system and stickers are not only colour coded but show the date of expiry of the system. Extensive research with helmet manufacturers and International Accident Research units has revealed that the standards reached in the manufacture of a helmet do not necessarily continue indefinitely.

Make sure that the helmets are stored properly within the car. Do not throw helmets on the back seat after a stage as they are a confounded nuisance rolling around inside the rear of the car and, in any case, it doesn't do them much good. Make a couple of boxes or brackets to carry the helmets but remember to position these so that you can reach them easily, preferably when wearing your seatbelts.

The engine noise inside a modern rally car is quite considerable and even worse when complemented by the sound of stones hitting the underside of the body. Therefore an intercom is desirable if the crew wish to communicate with each other clearly which, of course, they will when the co-driver is reading pace notes or route instructions to the driver. There must be no chance of an

instruction being misunderstood so a good two-way intercom is essential. Not only will the driver wish to hear a co-driver's route instructions, he may also wish to *give* instructions during the course of the stage. Some drivers will ask their co-drivers to switch on the windscreen wipers, the auxiliary fuel pump, or flick a fuel tank switch during an event.

Having selected the intercom, make sure it is expertly fitted or is an integral part of the helmet; holes bored in a helmet weaken it and even nullify the British Standard Institute certificate. If your intercom has a boom mike make sure that this is flexible and made of a soft material, otherwise you may lose your front teeth in an accident.

Most professional crews prefer an intercom which is fitted into their full-face helmets; the Swedish 'Peltor' model of intercom being extremely reliable. It is better if the co-driver or driver can hear himself through the intercom when he speaks to his partner because the co-driver will then tend to read pace notes and give instructions at the correct volume for easy listening (it will also prevent him from blowing out his driver's ear drums and, more importantly, let him *know* that he can be heard by the driver even if the engine noise level is high).

Although intercom systems were first developed for use with helmets, their use *without* helmets is now popular on road rallies. Although a road rally car should never be as noisy as a car built for stage events an intercom can be a useful asset as it saves the navigator having to shout all night, thus considerably easing stress.

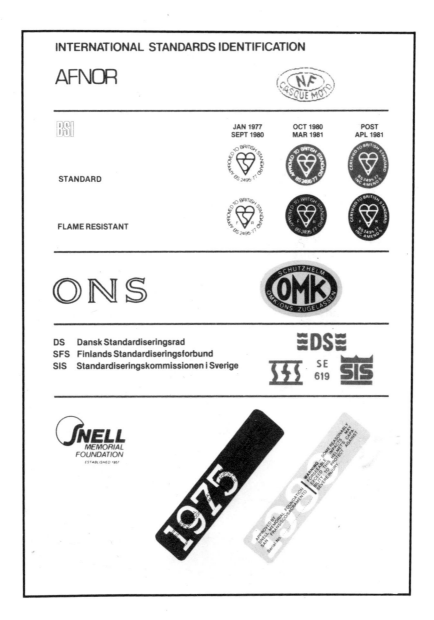

INTERNATIONAL STANDARDS IDENTIFICATION

AFNOR

BSI

	JAN 1977 SEPT 1980	OCT 1980 MAR 1981	POST APL 1981
STANDARD			
FLAME RESISTANT			

ONS

DS   Dansk Standardiseringsrad
SFS   Finlands Standardiseringsforbund
SIS   Standardiseringskommissionen i Sverige

SE 619

All these helmet standards are recognised by the RAC MSA at the time of publication.

HELMETS COMPLYING WITH BS 2495 (1977) SNELL 1975

HELMETS COMPLYING WITH BS 2495 (1977) SNELL 1975

HELMETS COMPLYING AFNOR S.72 302/303 BS 2495 (1977) AMT 5 ONS/OMK DIN 4848 DS, SFS, SIS, SNELL 1980

Crash helmets must be checked by Scrutineers and carry these approved stickers in Britain.
1) Red   2) and 3) Green

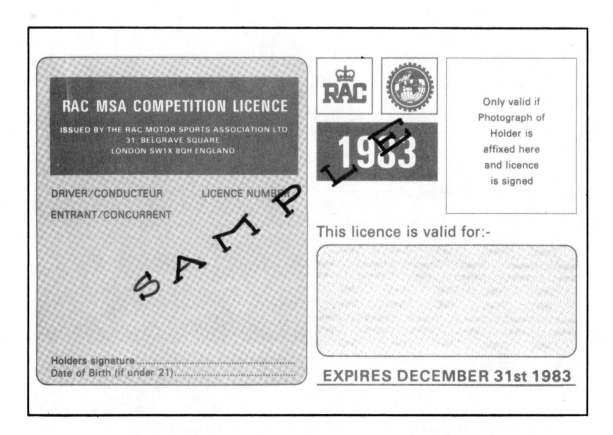

Another use of 'road rally style' headsets is during the practice or 'recce' for a rally, when it makes the job of writing and checking notes much easier. Crews also wear these headsets when driving on a road section of a stage rally or on a long, non special stage event such as the Safari Rally.

Fitting the intercom in the car is important; it must be securely mounted. If fitted to the roll cage (the ideal place as it can be switched on and off easily) see that it can't drop off during bumpy going. Make sure that all electrical connections are good and regularly inspected and ensure that the leads from the helmet have simple jack-plug ends so that they can be pulled out easily.

One piece of 'equipment' which every crew member must carry is a competition licence. This takes the form of a club membership card for 'closed-to-club' rallies or an R.A.C. licence for other events. Licence fees and qualification requirements alter from time to time but, as a guide.

Food and drink are of absorbing interest to most rally drivers, consequently navigators will find it one of their chores to 'feed and water' their drivers regularly. Although the days of picnic hampers laden with chicken legs and champagne have passed by, it

LICENCE FEES FOR RALLYING

Driver: (can also be entrant)	International	£ 28.00
	National	£ 15.00
	Restricted	£ 8.00
Navigator: (non-driver)	National	£ 15.00
	Restricted	£ 8.00
Advertising permits:	International	£170.00
	National	£ 80.00
	Restricted	£40.00
Trade entrants	All grades	£ 35.00

(all prices include VAT).

is necessary to carry a few tit-bits in a rally car because sensible food and drink can refresh a crew when its energy is waning.

Sandwiches and items that deteriorate are not a good idea nor are messy, crumbly or intricately wrapped foods. Most works drivers carry a small supply of boiled sweets, Polo mints, glucose tablets, chewing gum and possibly apples. Cheese can fall

A sample of an RAC MSA Competition Licence. Licences must be signed and carry a photograph of the holder to be valid.

into the 'messy' category but a number of drivers swear by it.

Take a bottle of orange squash, lemonade, glucose drink or mineral water but keep it tightly secured within the car and avoid very 'gassy' mineral waters as they are likely to cascade all over your car when the tops are removed.

A cup of hot coffee is an excellent reviver in the middle of the night but vacuum flasks seldom survive more than one rally so you may either rely on cafés kept open for controls by organisers or leave the supply of coffee to your service crew. Although the role of the service crew is dealt with in a later chapter, it is worth mentioning that a good service crew will always provide food and drink for its drivers. Works crews may enjoy soup, coffee, sandwiches, cheese, yoghurts, biscuits or whatever specialities they desire.

Some major factory teams have various hospitality coaches and caravans in which their drivers can be fed and watered. The Rothmans Opel team actually employed a *Cordon Bleu* cook at one time and many others employ specially trained people to supply food high in nutrition and energy-giving value.

Never be afraid or embarrassed about carrying personal items in the car. Some drivers carry a set of goggles in case the windscreen pops out, some carry a knife, a crowbar, sunglasses (very important), spare socks or a spare ignition key fastened to the zip of their rally jacket. You'd be surprised how many rally crews have incurred time penalties when they couldn't unlock their car after a control because they'd lost the ignition key!

Finally, if you have a lucky charm and think it makes you drive better then by all means carry it — confidence is half the battle and you'll need all the luck you can get anyway.

There's one more fairly important piece of equipment to consider of course — a car, so let us move on to the next chapter.

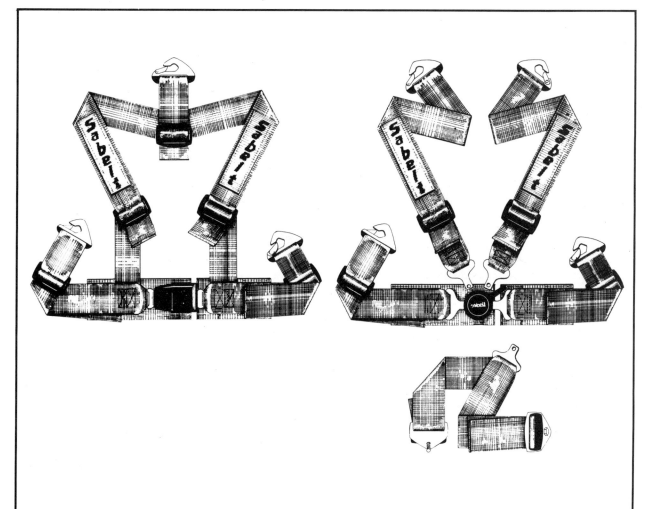

Good rally harnesses can be 3 or 4 point fixing and on the Sabelt 'Professional' model a 'crutch strap' is even offered for added security! Note the parachute-type quick release rotary buckle on the 'Professional' model or the quick release push button buckle on the 'Clubman' version.

5 Group therapy

When you first take up rallying on club events, almost any car will be eligible and you will be unlikely to face severe scrutineering. When choosing a car, don't buy anything way beyond your experience or ability – it will be costly and could be dangerous. Find out if the bug has *really* bitten you before you buy anything potent.

The classified columns of the enthusiast magazines offer some tempting machinery, but take care! It may be cheaper to start with an unmodified secondhand car that has had 'normal' usage and add lights, necessary safety items and so on to it, rather than buy a once glorious machine that is tired and at the end of its life.

If a car is advertised as having won its class on such-and-such a rally – so what? It's *your* driving ability that will count, not the previous owner's. There's quite a lot of tired old rubbish on offer so do get expert, down-to-earth advice if you are not mechanically minded.

Obviously *any* car you buy should comply with *legal* requirements but as you move up the competition tree on to more ambitious events, you will also have to pay attention to the *motor sport* regulations for vehicles allowed to take part in rallies.

Before a car can compete on a major event it must be 'homologated' for sporting purposes by the manufacturer. Homologation is not as painful as it sounds; it simply means the manufacturer lists the technical specification of a car on a Form of Recognition which also incorporates lots of photographs. The Form has to be signed by a senior official of the manufacturing company – as a check on honesty – and once the Form is validated, it becomes a virtual 'birth certificate' for the car; scrutineers can check a car against its Form to see that it complies with the rules.

The rules change from time to time and, in fact, a major switch in the early Eighties caused mild havoc.

As the regulations are relatively settled (and all things have to be 'relative' in the bizarre world of motor sport) it's worth making some attempt to understand the various groups which are currently allowed into rallies. They are as follows:

GROUP N

This is for large scale series production cars (at least 5000 built in twelve consecutive months) and was introduced in a desperate and worthy desire to see a 'bog standard' category, unmodified except for safety items such as brake pads and shoes and roll cages. Originally Group N was supposed to be a National formula (hence the 'N') with National clubs doing the homologation but some countries and manufacturers took it a bit more seriously than that. As a result Group N went "international" with a common form, leaving each country the option of producing their own forms for home use only. The risk is that the supposedly 'standard' Group N will gradually be relaxed so that it becomes very similar to the old Group 1. Moving up a stage, we come to:

GROUP A

Again this is intended for large scale production touring cars with at least 5000 built in twelve consecutive months but there is greater freedom for modifications than in Group N. Cars in Group A may be fettled through finishing and scraping, provided the original part can still be identified. Group A engine mods allow a free camshaft profile, but valve sizes and lift may not be changed. Chassis reinforcement is permitted and some sheet metal areas can be double-skinned. There is considerable freedom concerning suspension components, providing that the original geometry is retained and that the modified components appear in the homologation form. However, carburation must retain the standard system and, in general, the rules are tight enough to stop you turning a rogue car into a rally winner. The 'homologated' specification is critical — if the car hasn't got something in its basic spec (or at least listed on the form) then you can't use it!

Group A cars have minimum weight and rim widths stipulated according to capacity.

Finally, we have:

GROUP B

These are *limited* series production cars with a minimum of two seats. Two hundred have to be produced 'in twelve months and these are the 'supercars'. Considering their cost, some would say 'stupid' is a more appropriate word than 'super' and their fate when on their third or fourth owners may cause some concern. However, they do make a fine sight when in full cry in skilled hands. All the same freedoms are allowed as in Group A (alternative race or rally gearbox, reinforced drive shafts, suspension

components, two alternative final drive ratios, plus a higher ratio steering rack) as long as they appear in the homologation form. Slightly lower weight limits and rim/tyre rules allowing rims one inch wider than in Group A apply.

In the 'old' days it was possible to buy a car for, say, £10,000 and spend £20,000 on it to make it a rally winner. In theory under Group B you will pay £20,000 for a car and spend £10,000 on it; in other words the car has to be closer to standard when rallied. However, it's not exactly a bundle of fun for the amateur driver whichever way you look at it.

For all Groups there are rules about 'evolution' (under which an extra 10% of hotter cars can be built) but you've probably had enough by now so let us move on to consider how actually to prepare a rally car.

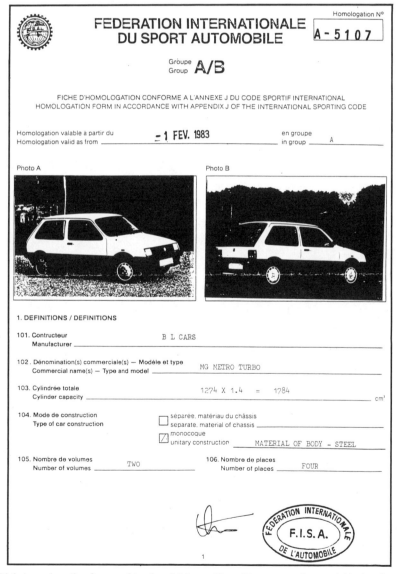

One page from an F.I.A. homologation form — virtually a 'birth certificate' for a car and essential before it can be used in major competition.

Just as Formula 1 teams spend a great deal of time testing, so do the major rally teams. Here we see the Ford Escort 1700T under development.

Make sure that you car conforms to the regulations and that you understand them – the scrutineers will.

Scrutineering can be an important – if somewhat longwinded – part of a major event.

6 Car preparation

Many sports need very little in the way of equipment – you *could* win an Olympic Gold Medal in your bare feet – but to get to the top, or even be moderately successful, in rallying, you will need a well-prepared car. But first – a word of caution: don't put a spanner anywhere near a rally car until you have squarely faced up to one or two questions:

How much can you afford to spend? A lot of rally programmes fizzle out part way through because the crew forgot to work out a proper budget.
What type of rallies are you proposing to enter? There is no point in spending money to build a car like a tank if you are going to concentrate on smooth, tarmac rallies.
Are you really certain that you are Britain's answer to the Scandinavians? Really sure? Because if you aren't then it doesn't make sense to build a full-blooded – and very, very expensive – works replica. Far too many people waste money preparing cars which are way ahead of their driving ability.

So, having done our best to disillusion you, let us now move on to discuss just how you can best set out to prepare your rally car.

Study the regulations. That is simple to say but from the clangers people drop it would seem to be difficult for some people to do.

Study the regulations for your type of rallying and study the homologation form for your car until you are quite sure you know exactly what you are allowed to do. In particular it is unforgivable to be caught cheating in one of the 'one-make' rally championships. Experience has shown that in those series the odd 2 or 3bhp doesn't make a blind bit of difference so it just isn't worth sailing close to the edge of the regulations to gain them.

Remember that if your car is new then doing any motor sport in it will almost certainly clobber your warranty!

Before you start work, try to talk to one or two people running the same make of car – they should be able to alert you to any pitfalls.

Do you have any mechanical skill? If not, but can find a friend to help you work on the car, then it is worth tackling your own preparation. At one time the works teams were happiest with drivers with little mechanical knowledge; not so nowadays when testing and general sorting is so important in rallying – just as it is in Formula 1. If you do your own work on your rally car you will be more capable of fixing it during an event.

What workshop space do you have? Marriages have been broken by engine rebuilds under the bed. Remember that a stripped rally car can take up a lot of space. And *if* you have the time and money that is how you should start: by stripping your car down to the shell. *Not* essential of course, and you may win rallies just by bolting on a couple of extra lights, but you will be absolutely *sure* of your car if it has had a total rebuild.

This is the time to do any welding or cutting and shutting – such as putting a fireproof bulkhead behind the rear seats.

Whatever your budget limitations, you must not cut corners on safety items.

So now fit an interior roll cage and make it a full-house version with tubes down the windscreen pillars. Pad the cage wth rubber and cover any protruding bolts.

While you have the car stripped down, do what you can to block off holes so that the car stays fairly free from dust and water during a rally.

Next, the area which loses more rallies than anything else; the electrics. Sit quietly with a large sheet of paper and *plan* what is going to go where on your car and sort out your wiring accordingly. Always use the correct specification of wire for a particular load and obviously vary the colours so that you can identify things.

Don't ramble wires around the car; keep things

as neat and tidy as possible. Use grommets wherever necessary and avoid sharp edges. The list goes on; connections need to be grease free and tight; battery terminals should be kept clean; fuseboxes should be accessible: fit relays to the horn and extra lamps to reduce the voltage drop. In other words *pay attention to detail.*

You may well decide to uprate the alternator; if so, make sure you fit the correct bracket etc, because this is a vulnerable area. If you *do* change the alternator don't forget to have the control box and regulator checked to suit the power and the battery – over-charging can be nearly as big a headache as undercharging.

If your wife or girl friend hasn't strangled you with a jump lead by now and you have a car with impeccable wiring, start putting the suspension back so that you can get the car onto its wheels. Don't start experimenting with suspensions, fit whatever the leading drivers use who run your type of car. It is too early in your career to get neurotic over suspension settings.

Make very sure that the bump stops work before the shock absorbers are fully compressed, otherwise you will damage the brackets or, worse, the turrets.

Spring rates and ride heights will be controlled to some extent by the type of rallies you are doing; as a general rule attempts to jack-up cars into the sky cause all sorts of other problems and aren't successful. Anyway you will be protecting your engine wth one of the most important fittings: a sump guard. Get a good one and fit it properly. If you fit an expensive lightweight sump guard add a sheet of thin mild steel to it – it will be cheaper to replace this now and again if appropriate than to buy a new guard.

Use heavy duty bushes where available and fit a high ratio steering rack; don't underestimate the arm effort needed for modern high speed rallying.

RL 33

A good roll-over bar is essential

Install the most appropriate final drive you can afford. Drivers always want low ratios, team managers like to play safe with high. The drivers are usually proved right!

We nearly forgot: fit a limited slip diff of course if appropriate but *only* if it is allowed under the regulations. It is a very easy thing for a scrutineer to check!

If the cost of all this is starting to frighten you, bear in mind that if you are an undiscovered genius then you may be able to shine in your aunt's old shopping car, but it is unlikely. You just have to accept that motor sport of any sort is going to cost you money!

So let us spend some more of your money and consider the clutch. Most standard clutches have a certain safety margin – say 10% or so – so if you are leaving your engine standard your clutch should cope. Better though to fit a competition one. Considering how much more reliable they make rally cars, competition clutches are quite cheap and are usually interchangeable with the standard ones.

Having taken some trouble with your axle (such as by having the best available halfshafts) and fitted a competition clutch, now get your propshaft properly balanced before fitting it.

Remember what we said about not economising on safety? Well, here we go again because the next item to consider is the brakes. Brake pipes must be well protected and run inside the car where possible. The flexible hoses should have protective springs coiled round them. Washers and seals should be replaced regularly – an advantage of doing your own maintenance and preparation is that you will get a feel for when this should be. Discs and drums must be running true, wheel bearings must be checked regularly, drums should be cleaned out regularly and you need competition brake fluid. All obvious things, but all important.

If you have a dual-line braking system with one cylinder operating the front brakes and another the rear you will, if the cylinders have an adjustable swinging beam between them, be able to 'tune' the balance of the braking between front and rear. *But,* ladies and gentleman, this is for experts – don't waste time or money on such sophistication until you are very, very sure that you are capable of making use of it.

With only mild power increases you should be able to stop OK if you simply fit competition brake material. Bed the pads and/or shoes in as advised by the manufacturer and if you expect to have to change during an event, bed a spare set in beforehand. If a material change isn't enough to give you proper stopping power then **consult an expert** before you venture into a complete system change – we don't want to lose you (we need someone to buy our next book)!

The roll-over bar should be padded to protect the crew in an accident. Note the flexible map light mounted to the bar.

Modify the handbrake to give it a fly-off action.

Wheels? Well, a lot of people get carried away by cosmetics and fit wheels which may be prettier but are in fact heavier than standard, which is silly. Simple advice: follow the advice of people who are winning in your car. Don't go overboard on rim widths.

Happily, some of the one-make rally championships are stipulating one type of tyre. Sensible, because tyre permutations and costs have done more damage to rallying than perhaps we realise. When you hear works teams talk of 600 tyres for a three car team on a Monte, perhaps it is time for a still, small voice to cry "enough"?

Because of the competition between manufacturers — which can only benefit the clubman — it would be dangerous in this book to give advice on particular tyres because things change so quickly. Our only advice is not to burden yourself with the cost of umpteen tyre permutations until your driving deserves them. Once again — ask the leading competitors for advice but this time probe them on the puncture record of particular tyres — in your early stages you want to have trouble-free rallies while

you shake yourself down; you won't get them if you are constantly changing wheels because of punctures.

Anyway, now you should have a well prepared shell, fitted with a sump guard and safety cage and with a well sorted axle, prop-shaft, gearbox, etc, (we will come to the engine later). And presumably at some stage you will have had the car painted. Although rallying has improved its image over the years with the growth of sponsorship, there are still very few cars *properly* presented with eye catching colour schemes. Give it a thought and if you or a mate have got styling flair you may attract attention simply because you have a well presented car. Remember too that the cleaner and crisper your car looks, the better ride you may have with scrutineers.

Now let us move inside the car. Seats are a matter for personal preference. They should be strong and firmly bolted down with zero play. The fore and aft position should be tailored for the number one driver.

Back to safety, fit the best seat belts you can get and **fit them properly**. You will get bounced about a lot on special stages so you must be able to 41

Mount the seats firmly and fit full safety harnesses.

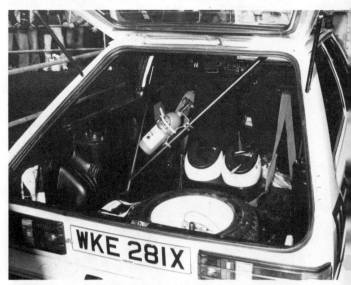

Fit some form of crash hat carrier – like the one shown here.

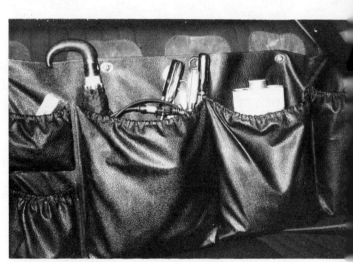

A pouch on the back seat makes a good home for tools and spares. Note also the umbrella in case of breakdown, when the crew may have to walk!

strap yourself in firmly. The co-driver will probably want to sit well back in the car (out of your way as you do your Hero Driver bit) in which case a bracing bar for his feet will be necessary so that he can push himself into his seat as he sits there counting his beads.

When did you last have an instrument fail in a standard car? Probably never. Which is a good argument for not loading your rally car with a battery of extra dials. You should have an oil gauge or warning light of course; adjust it so that you get a warning *before* any damage is done.

The co-driver will need a plug for his light which brings us into the realm of ergonomics (the word adds a touch of culture to the book if nothing else). Get with your co-driver and sit in the car and then decide where you are going to place his plug, any auxiliary switches, a torch holder, crash hat supports and so on. Don't mount extra switches in groups of more than three – there is a limit to how far most drivers can count.

Additional lights sometimes fall into the area of machismo. Fit what you are allowed; fit the best; mount them so that they won't wobble about; wire them properly – then forget them. Don't blame the lights if you get murdered on every night stage, find out first if you are one of those people who simply hasn't got very good night vision. Make sure additional lights comply with the law.

Incidentally, if you are serious about saving weight (and you should be) you could perhaps have quick release plugs for auxiliary lights so that they can be removed on daylight sections (provided the regulations allow this) and carried in a support car. Only do this if it can be organised without any hassle.

Back to our ergonomics, neatness must be the watchword. Stow everything safely and carry this theory back to the boot too. Don't allow a heavy spare wheel to fly about, nor a battery for that matter which can be even more dangerous. If your boot needs a key to open it, wire one in place during a rally to save time. A safety petrol tank is nice to have, though costly of course. Locking petrol caps should be replaced before a rally – they waste time. Add bonnet clips to stop it flying up or working loose – the same for the boot.

You must naturally have a fire extinguisher on board and the car must have a clearly marked external switch for the electrical circuit so that a

Instrumentation may be kept to a minimum on a road rally car as these two photographs show.

Be neat in the boot too. Make sure that the spare wheel cannot bounce about.
The engine compartment must be given maximum attention.

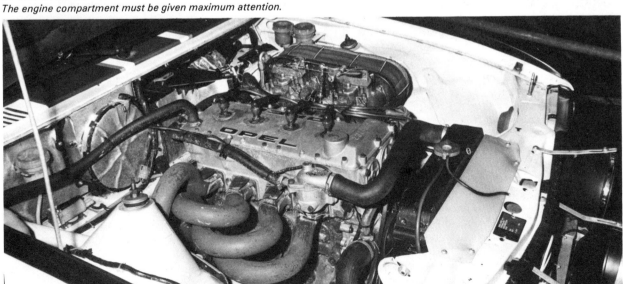

The engine compartment of a road rally car will be a lot simpler and more straightforward but will still need to be neat and tidy and meticulously prepared.

Having spent money on the engine, protect it with a good sump guard.

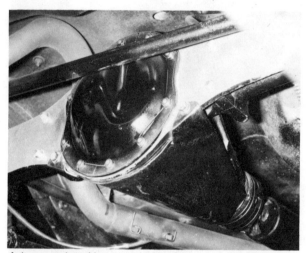

Axles are vulnerable — note the bracing bar and skid plate fitted to this one.

Skids on the silencer will help to protect it from damage. Adequate silencing is essential if rallying is to avoid antagonising the public.

spectator can operate it if, for instance, you are trapped in a car after a shunt.

You will need a tow rope. Oh yes you will. If you leave the back seat out you can replace it with a canvas or plastic sheet with stowage pockets and carry a tow rope in there — along with spare wiper blades, tyre levers and (for events a fair way from home) a spare gasket set.

With all the weight you have added there is something to be said for leaving the carpets at home. The car will be noisier but will be as noisy as hell anyway with stones being hurled about underneath on forest stages. Having saved that weight, put a bit back by carrying a first aid kit.

Nearly finished the preparation saga now, but there is still one thing to consider — the engine. Eric Carlsson made a bigger impact on rallying in his day than anyone and he weighed 18 stone and his Saab had a tiny engine. In the old Mexico championship, whenever Peter Ashcroft put a few cars on a rolling

road he often found the winners were a few bhp down on the rest. If it is dark, cold and wet and you are going downhill on a loose surface then power to weight is less important than driving ability, far less; which is a long winded way of saying don't waste money on engine tuning until your driving is up to it.

A basic but worthwhile improvement can be gained by simply stripping the engine and having it rebuilt under what is picturesquely called blueprinting, in other words getting everything to the best tolerance for performance. Combustion chambers can be balanced and equalised; manifolds and ports can be matched precisely and so on. Probably more trouble than it is worth for average rallying — more relevant to production car racing perhaps, but if you do it you may *feel* the car is quicker and have more confidence as a result (and confidence is half the battle) and at least the stripping and rebuilding will give you an intimate knowledge of your engine.

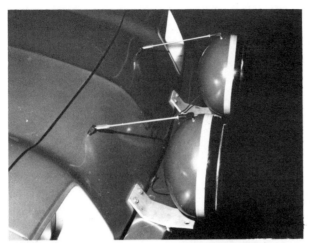

Spotlights flapping about do not give the driver confidence. Note the adjustable support bars and the sturdy brackets.

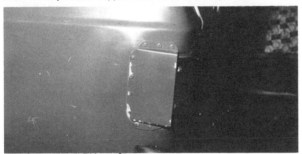

Here's a neat idea for the club rally driver who's frightened of losing his rear lights if he should accidentally clip a wall or tree with the back end.

Fire extinguishers must be of the correct type and mounted properly.

Try to keep the interior as neat as possible – note the extra door pockets for the co-driver of this Audi Quattro.

Whichever way you plan to tackle fords, you must waterproof your car. Above, Bjorn Waldegaard on New Zealand's Motogard Rally and below traffic congestion on the Newtown Eagle Rally in Wales.

The early rally pictures in this book featured no sponsors' advertising. All that has changed! Lamp covers are a 'high exposure' area.

Prime advertising sites are the bonnets ...

... and even the bumper.

If you get involved in more elaborate engine tuning we recommend that you aim for mid-range torque rather than out and out top-end performance. It may be impressive at the bar to mention casually a high bhp figure but if it is only achieved at very high revs (and your gearing means that you only reach it after seven miles flat-out on Pendine Sands) it won't exactly do you much good on plot and bash rallies. But then not too many rallies are won at the bar nowadays, otherwise the results tables would be vastly different.

The key phrase under more general tuning is 'machining and polishing' because if the regulations permit you can clearly improve engine performance by raising compression and generally improving the gas flow. But — and we hate to keep preaching but we *are* trying to save you money — go for reliability and when possible copy the experts (and in your

47

case an 'expert' should be regarded as someone who finishes fairly well up regularly i.e., with a reliable car).

Rallying has its opponents and noise is quoted as one of the sport's most irritating features, so fit a good exhaust system and make sure it will stay in place. You have decided to take up rallying so that you can have a roarty car to impress the birds? Well, we admire your rather muddled motives but could you possibly clear-off and take up another sport?

Even a standard exhaust system will have a longer life if you strengthen it with a support bracket taken off the bellhousing: you should also tack weld all the joints in the system to keep it in one piece. Add 'skids' of mild steel strip to each end of the silencer box — as well as at any other vulnerable points — to stop the box being knocked off on rocks. Sooner or later you will have to reverse in a fairly narrow space; if your exhaust pipe sticks out at the back it will get filled with earth. Keep it short.

In theory the car should now be nearly ready for its first event. But pause. Go over the car carefully.

Any bolts sticking out where they can catch against a pipe or wire? Any bolts sticking out which could catch against *you* if you roll over? Any brackets which you bodged-up in a hurry and which spoil the overall look of the car? Remake them.

Jack, tools, wheelbrace, first aid kit, sweeties all carefully stowed? Sponsor's stickers neatly displayed?

Can you get full throttle?

When you are satisfied on all these things take your baby out, grit your teeth and drive it in anger over a local rough road. Go on, force yourself. If it won't survive a couple of miles of this, how do you expect it to survive a rally?

Often things which are going to come loose will do so in the first couple of miles — better that these are test miles, rather than on an actual event. When you get back from the test run, check everything again, then wash and polish the car before you report to the start of a rally.

Some events allow service. Many argue against it — including at times the works teams who are horrified at the cost of helicopters and planes on Safaris and such like.

If you are on a rally and works teams are present *don't* expect the works mechanics to mother you. They will have different priorities. In fact the only real way to grab their attention is to go so well that you end up beating the works cars. But it ain't easy.

If you put out your own service car *please* do not set it high average speeds between service points. Too many mechanics have had accidents that way.

48   *The amount of advertising on this Lancia barely leaves room for the number plate!*

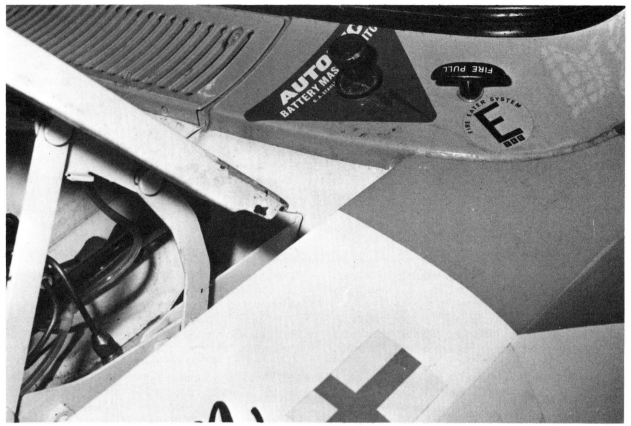

Switches for the battery mains and fire extinguisher must be readily accessible outside the car in case the crew are trapped in an accident.

Regulations require crew names to be painted outside the car on international events. On club rallies it is not a requirement and may be as well when there are frequent navigation changes!

7 Rally driving

Have you had a medical check recently? Are your eyes O.K.? If you wear glasses have you had them checked lately?

All points worth considering before you try to become a rally driver. Not much point in spending a lot of money on extra lights if your eyes need testing. Not much point in shaving a few grams off the weight of your car if you've got a bulbous belly.

Don't get us wrong – you don't have to be a superman to do well on rallies and certainly you don't have to be as fit as say, a marathon runner or sprinter. But consider for a moment ... the standard of competition is high so doesn't it make sense to get yourself in the best possible shape before you start rallying?

If nothing else, if you are fit you will be better able to push your car out of a forest if you have a breakdown.

One other thing before you start rally driving. Have you been to one of the rally schools? Worth doing because although you may have to lay out £60 or so, it is better to do this than to spend a lot more on preparing a car only to find that you have little or no basic aptitude. If you make this unhappy discovery but decide to plough on, at least the knowledge can steer you in the right direction on cars and preparation.

One rather important benefit of a rally school is that it will give you a chance to sit with a star driver and study his technique.

Having decided to continue, you now need to get yourself into gear – overalls, crash hat, gloves, shoes and so on. No need to go berserk on your equipment at the beginning but let us repeat what we said in an earlier chapter: make sure clothing is practical and comfortable. Don't wear anything new for the first time on an event; if your new fireproof underpants choke you (you may have your own priorities on what you want to protect) find out before, not on, a rally. We made the point in car preparation that the sport needs smart presentation so please don't turn up at the start of a rally in greasy, torn overalls. Keep an old pair for working on the car, a better pair for driving in.

Medical experts reckon that it takes up to thirty minutes for your eyes to adjust to darkness after being in bright lights ... so carry sunglasses to put on at night controls, where there may be TV lights and photographers' flash guns. Obviously you will also need the sunglasses on bright days. Night driving glasses are not recommended.

Once you have fitted yourself out with proper clothing and equipment, you need to blend yourself with your car. Can you reach all the controls when you are strapped in? Are you happy with the pedals? Is the seat mounted properly for you? Most drivers seem happier with more of a sit-up-and-beg driving position than that adopted by racing drivers – it obviously helps to be able to see enough to 'place' a car. Don't have the seat ludicrously high of course, otherwise you will end up as the Hunchback of Knotty Ash!

If you like a steering wheel with a turquoise, sheepskin cover then fit it, duckie, but don't expect it to make you any quicker. There is really not much wrong with standard steering wheels but if you feel happier with something different – be our guest.

Remember that a steering wheel is not intended as an additional grab handle, just for steering.

Don't bother too much with fine tuning the suspension and brakes until you have a little experience, nor should you become obsessive about tyre pressures.

You may have your own views on how you want to set your lights – clearly they mustn't irritate non-competing cars coming the other way – but do remember to set the lights with car fully laden in *rally trim*.

That means with your co-driver onboard. This poor devil is the guy who can rarely win a rally for you, but he can certainly lose one, so choose

Hannu Mikkola has been winning for two decades. Although as authors we should be impartial, we have to say that in our opinion Mikkola is 'the tops!'

Do put your daughter on the stage Mrs. Worthington! This is Michele Mouton, the fastest female driver in the world and the first to equal the great rally achievements of the legendary Pat Moss some twenty years earlier.

him/her with care. In fact in your early days it is worth doing a rally or two as a navigator yourself, this will give you some idea of the problems the co-driver faces and therefore the qualities you need to look for in one. Several top drivers, including Michèle Mouton, started as navigators. If you are totally without experience then you are not going to get the star co-drivers leaping into your car so you will just have to look for someone who is pleasant to get on with and, hopefully, a disciplined thinker and good at figures. Note that "pleasant to get on with" is listed first. Let's face it: rallying is a sport which should be done for fun — why put up with a miserable sod just because he is a good co-driver?

Can your proposed co-driver drive? Will you be able to rest while he steers you from one special stage to another? Has he driving ambitions of his own? (if so turn through 180 degrees and run away as fast as you can).

Can he/does he write for any of the motoring papers? If so it may help you to get assistance from overseas rallies which may be glad of media coverage.

Now you have sorted out yourself and your car and found a co-driver, don't set off for a rally just yet. Practise first.

Go out over local roads (at night) and shake yourself down as a crew. Get used to each other's language (it may get colourful under stress). Practise wheel changing; few crews do but it can save vital seconds on a stage if you know where everything is stowed and who is going to do what during the wheel change. And practise wearing full rally gear including crash hats!

Watch some of the tops works pairings in action — or for that matter the more professional road rally crews — and you'll begin to appreciate what the sport is about.

By this stage you should have enough confidence to concentrate on how to become a better driver, safe in the knowledge that you have taken care as far as possible of all the factors contributing to success — the car, co-driver, etc.

And if you want to become a star driver (or simply a competent clubman) then it sounds obvious but as we said earlier there is one thing you must do above all else and that is *drive*. Drive everything and anything at every opportunity. Hannu Mikkola had a season of saloon car racing based on Rochdale (very character forming) and it put an edge on his driving. We are not suggesting you need a full season of club racing but certainly a

A pensive Jimmy McRae ...

... and the ever cheerful John Buffum, the USA's top rally driver

few races will give you a wider appreciation of speed. Autotests, rallycross, autocross – anything; if it has four wheels and an engine, then drive it.

Keep records. In other words log all the events you do, making a note of other competitors and how you fared against them (so that you can see if you are improving if you meet them later). Log where you finished, how many starters, how well the event was run, any marshalling problems, any difficulty in getting hotels, any problems in finding the start, and so on and so on and so on. The sort of thing which will help you to do better on the rally the following year.

There is something to be said for a season or so of *road* events before you tackle the tougher stage rallies – it will certainly bed you in as a crew. When you do get onto stage events you will quickly realise the obvious: rallies are won or lost on corners. Given the right sized wellie anyone can drive fast in a straight line. You must learn to corner well.

The technique is obviously governed by the road surface. If you are on dry tarmac then the neatness of a racing driver is appropriate. Incidentally, note how most of the sideways Formula One men eventually settle down to a more controlled line. And a smooth line is particularly important with the lower-powered one-make cham-

pionships – hurl the car about too much and you will scrub off all your speed!

But even if the road is dry and the sun is shining and the birds are singing you must cultivate one thing: *determination.*

You must want to win. You must want to will the blasted car to the end of the stage. You must shut your mind to anything but that one objective, getting the car to the finish as fast as possible.

Experience at the Ford Rally School indicated that people just will not *concentrate.* It's not easy to maintain concentration and determination when it's cold, wet and windy and you've just had a puncture but maintaining concentration is the key to success.

If you concentrated when on tarmac, you will have to concentrate just as hard on loose surfaces. If you are enough of an enthusiast to have bought this book and waded this far you will probably have seen one of the excellent rally films there are about. If so you will have noticed one thing: cars don't always go round corners in a conventional fashion. The back ends of the cars are swinging this way and that.

This is because if you drive round a loose corner in the conventional way, as you speed up you will understeer off the road. Note when the first ice of winter hits the country how many people slide off into ditches on the outside of bends; in other words they have understeered off. The same thing will happen on a loose special stage unless you set up the car to stop it. Purists may argue that you could tune suspensions to remove the understeer but they forget that the surfaces are loose and sometimes rough, which tends to clobber the theory.

If you are approaching a left-hand bend on a loose surface and deliberately put the car into an unstable situation by a sharp turn on the steering wheel to the right, you will then be able to flick or 'pendulum' the car back round to the left to go round the corner and because of the controlled (at least we hope it is controlled) instability you will avoid going off through understeer. It may look like one long accident looking for somewhere to happen when you see it for the first time, but it can be safer and faster. Obviously humps and bumps may throw you off your intended line in the middle of a corner so you must be ready to correct immediately. Don't overdo the see-sawing about of course if it results in scrubbing too much speed off. It is all a question of balance and control and, of course, experience.

The ability to have a car under control on a loose surface is the key to success on special stages. At the rally schools you will find yourself asked to drive round and round a single pylon — holding the car on line with throttle control. This not only teaches car control — it makes people realise that you have to work hard and concentrate.

If all else fails and a slide off the road seems inevitable you still have one friend left: the handbrake. If you are doing 25mph or so, then yank on the steering wheel and at the same time de-clutch and tug at the handbrake (which should be the fly-off type) you will find, to your co-driver's surprise (and possibly yours) that you have turned through 180 degrees. And it can be done in roads

only slightly wider than the car is long. Both authors during misspent youths as navigators have overshot turnings and been pivoted through 180 degrees by drivers doing handbrake turns.

Don't practise it on public roads. Find somewhere quiet and loose and keep doing it until you can judge the right amount of effort and sharpness to put into your actions. Once you have mastered it you can use the technique to spin to a stop if you are in danger of going off and, with practice, you will be able to use the handbrake to induce the instability we talked about and hence help your general cornering particularly on hairpins. Caution though — don't get neurotic about it, concentrate on your general driving technique first.

And the same applies to the dreaded left-foot braking, which mainly applies to front-wheel-drive cars. It is a much discussed technique and can work well but you *must* practise and practise again to make a success of it.

The big problem with front-wheel-drive cars when driven in anger is that as you apply the power the front wheels may lose their grip, which in turn induces understeer, which can be terminal if you don't do something about it. The Scandinavians worked out that if you keep your right foot on the accelerator and put your left foot on the brake you can control the rear wheels through the braking system, while your right foot (and hopefully the steering too of course) controls the front end. Using the left foot on the brakes makes the back end come round, just as the handbrake does. For the same reason most drivers have their brakes biased towards the rear.

The brakes being on while the accelerator is pressed can also act as something of a limited slip, although if you are too enthusiastic with the left foot you will simply slow yourself down.

Bear in mind that unless you are very careful you will burn out your brakes and be no quicker, so let us repeat: only try it when you have explored and mastered the other techniques. Try to see the old Castrol film of the Flying Finns which features Timo Makinen demonstrating the technique in a Mini. He makes it quite clear that you have to change gear without using the clutch, which may be less than appealing if you are buying your own gearboxes!

In theory you can use the same left foot technique on front engined, rear-wheel-drive cars but it must be stressed that more rallies are won without using it. The idea is that it helps you to balance a car better and that in particular it can help you take off properly before a brow so that you 'fly' at the right angle.

Incidentally if a brow is 'blind' try not to approach it in a straight line. The Scandinavians work on the reasonable theory that if someone has taken the trouble to build a road through a forest and up a hill, then presumably they have continued

The pedals must be adjusted until the driver is completely happy with them. Note the support for the left foot — don't use the clutch as a resting place!

A cross-section of Pirelli's new, softer sidewall construction and tread compound rally tyre developed from its Formula One programme.

On the left, is a selection of Pirelli's P7 M & S tyres, with their multi-angled block tread patterns which present biting edges in all directions, therefore the tyres are ideal for loose surfaces.

Designed for very rough forest stages, hard surfaces and ice are the hard compound Pirelli P7 SG 35 variants (right bottom two). For tarmac stages (right, top three), Pirelli offers the choice of intermediate, rain and the famous "Thermal" slick, all with a new 'super soft' compound for improved handling.

the road on the other side of the hill *but* (and there so often is a 'but' in rallying) there may be a T-junction just the other side. If you fly majestically over the brow pointing straight ahead, you may well exit from the rally through the fence which is also straight ahead.

If you come over with the car slightly out of line (in the unstable position we talked about earlier) then you will be better placed to flick the car round the corner.

We are all happy that all this is taking place on roads closed to other traffic aren't we ...? Good.

If you wake up one morning and the roads are covered in snow, don't go back to bed. Get out and practise.

We see snow so rarely in Britain that it makes sense to use every opportunity to get the feel of driving on it. You will need to use similar techniques

to driving on the loose and the same applies to sheet ice of course. Note by the way that under slippery conditions, top drivers will de-clutch if all is lost. Removing the drive from the wheels makes things as smooth as possible and may keep you in control of the situation. Practise this if possible.

On a rally in snow your running order is critical, as is the track of your car. If you have a different track to everyone else you may find yourself having to master virgin snow all the time.

For known snowy conditions you may on some events be allowed to use studded tyres. Our advice? Ask the tyre companies if they have any good secondhand studded tyres left over from previous years and use those. The top drivers will sometimes get into a sweat over this make of stud or that type of bonding – just as skiers argue over the best type of preparation for their skis – but when

Part of the Audi team's tyre stock prior to a major event. Note the crayon markings to indicate grooves which will be hand cut.

the chips or flakes are down it all hinges on how quick the driver is.

What else? Oh yes. Fog! Horrid stuff but you will meet it sooner or later. No known technique for seeing through it. If someone passes you, try to hang on to them, at the risk of following the District Nurse into her drive.

In Formula One it seems to be an accepted tactic to make it difficult for another driver to get past. Not so in rallying. If someone catches you up it means they are quicker than you are, so get out of the way as soon as you can. *Never* baulk other cars.

It is a few pages since we last mentioned it so let us remind you again: *concentrate.* Concentrate in fog. Concentrate in rain and don't forget to concentrate on *easy* road sections. If you are chatting about your heroic performance on the last stage some of the shine will be taken off if you hit the back of a milk-float through not paying attention.

In the split of duties the driver should really be the one in touch with the mechanical needs of the car so as you are running into a fuel stop, control or overnight halt, dictate a list of 'jobs to be done' to the co-driver. And try to give things an order of priority. The fact that your jelly-baby holder has come loose is slightly less important than that the exhaust is falling off. If, sadly, you are faced with a

major job – such as a gearbox change – the co-driver should be working out exactly how much time will be in hand both before and *after* the stop, while you think through how to tackle the job.

With experience you should be able to pace yourself. We say "should" although this does seem to take some of the young Scandinavians a long time.

Learn when to pull out all the stops and above all learn never to give up. If you make a porridge of a stage, keep going – the stage may be cancelled for some reason.

Never give up unless of course you have a major accident. And you need to recognise that if you are trying hard and hoping to go places, then sooner or later you are going to have an accident. Rallying is a relatively safe sport but there are no special techniques for having happy accidents, although it does seem as if some drivers bear charmed lives – or have such developed reflexes that they can stay in touch with things later than lesser mortals.

Don't misunderstand us – we are *not* advocating an irresponsible approach which puts you in a ditch on every rally. What we are saying is that if you are to find your limit then sooner or later you are likely to overcook things and come unstuck.

How you learn from the experience and how you progress as a result will dictate just how good a driver you become.

Two final points on rally driving: **never** try to improve your performance by taking drugs. They are unlikely to make you quicker, they could mar your judgement and cause an accident. And most impor-

tant of all, rallying just doesn't need the drug taking scandals which beset other sports.

Finally, avoid driving with windows open – a major cause of injury in crashes according to rally medical officers; the temptation (foolishly) to put your arm out to stop a car turning over is very strong – and very dangerous!

Rally drivers must be versatile. Here's Tony Pond on the Lombard RAC ...

... Per Eklund in New Zealand ...

... Ian Cathcart in Ireland

... and Terry Benson on a Lakeland road rally.

Even at 3am. spectators turn out in their hundreds to watch club road rallies. This picture shows Dave Wilkes and Simon Slade negotiating a hairpin on a South West Championship event.

Slippery conditions in the West Country for a typical road rally crew.

8 Rally navigation

Having devoted a chapter to developing the *prima ballerinas* it is now time to introduce the *corps de ballet,* that brave body always destined to play the role of bridesmaids, the poor little Cinderellas hidden away from the limelight – the navigators or co-drivers!

The navigator/co-driver enjoys little of the glamour but most of the worries, (ever counted the number of co-drivers with grey hair/no hair/ulcers?). At the professional level the co-driver only earns a fraction of the top drivers' fees yet frequently finds himself the subject of abuse and criticism and ends up with all the dirty jobs.

In the event of a breakdown it will be the co-driver who walks for miles over frozen moorland to summon help whilst the driver sleeps in a cosy rug. Before the rally it will be the co-driver who sits in his hotel room checking his pace-notes and studying the regulations while the driver goes to a glittering pre-rally reception to meet Miss World. After being thrown about and pummelled on the rally it will be the co-driver who misses the post-rally dinner because he is checking the results. Blessed are the meek.

The sole redeeming feature of navigating is that it is the cheapest way into the sport, and if you're lucky enough to reach the very top and sit alongside the world's great drivers as part of a Works Team you'll appreciate the privileged position you occupy; all the horrors and hardships will have been worth it.

However, before we discuss the craft at which you'll need to become perfect, let us briefly discuss the terminology used in describing the poor creature, for he doesn't even possess a proper title!

Basically the navigator tends to be so-called when he's conducting the map work on a road event and where he will never be expected to touch the steering wheel. Co-drivers were originally called such on the bigger Internationals where navigation was not too difficult and where they might be required to drive, albeit on easier sections.

Now the term co-driver is used for the passenger on even the smallest stage event when there is absolutely no likelihood of his taking the wheel. On anything but a navigational road rally we should really describe him as the Office Manager for that is what he is – a highly organised office manager who can drive safely (if he has to give his precious partner a rest) and who probably has a good knowledge of psychology, mathematics, languages, geography and economics. If you qualify on all counts, telephone your nearest team manager immediately. If you fail to qualify, don't worry, we've yet to find anyone who does.

A good navigator (and we'll call him that for the rest of this chapter) will start by gaining as much experience as possible in every type of event from the smallest treasure hunt upwards. He will be a keen motor club member – probably be involved in running events and committee work as all this develops the ability to organise, which is the navigator's job. By helping organise rallies one begins to understand the workings of organisers' minds and this can be very useful for a competitor.

The navigator will be a tidy-minded individual and will keep everything in its place in the car, and although he will let the driver look after the mechanical bits he will know where the jack, the spare fuses and the tow-rope are stowed.

Now on to the navigator's equipment.

The most important, and probably the first item to be purchased by a navigator will be a map. Assuming you are starting in British rallies this will inevitably come from the glorious range of Ordnance Survey Maps, most likely one of the 1:50,000 series; these give a scale of approximately $1\frac{1}{4}$ inches to the mile and are used by all British rally organisers. The organisers of any rally will specify the maps to be used on the event, and you should obtain these maps in good time and prepare them for the rally.

Ordnance Survey Maps are available in folded or unfolded form, and it is a matter of personal

The driver can help his navigator by reading out route instructions and map references.

Navigators should always make it as easy as possible for marshals. Note the light above the door which the navigator will switch on at each control.

preference which you use. Most people take folded versions as they are easier to store and file.

When you buy your Ordnance Survey Map you will notice that it is covered by thin lines forming small squares — these lines are part of the National Grid which covers the country and is based on a point in the English Channel, south-west of Land's End. The figures by the lines along the edges of the map represent their distances in kilometres, east and north of this origin. If total measurements from the point off Lands End were taken, the number of kilometres would be too large for practical use, so the figures are repeated every 100 kilometres and each 100 kilometre square is designated by two letters. The small diagram on the bottom of each map shows the incidence of grid letters on it. You will rarely, if ever, encounter the letters on a rally, the actual map being indicated by its number and you'll become very familiar with these map numbers and know that sheet 136 is "Newtown and Llanidloes", sheet 95 is the Isle of Man and so on.

When plotting a map reference always plot 'eastings' first; these are the numbers printed along the top and bottom edges of the map. Next plot the 'northings' — the numbers printed down both sides. There are several catch phrases to help you to remember which to plot first, one of the more printable being "along the passage and up the stairs". In other words, first look *along* the bottom edge, then *up* the sides. To make it easier to plot a reference, every tenth grid line is printed slightly heavier than the rest. In a six figure reference the

first three figures represent tens, units and tenths of kilometres east and the last three represent those to the north (see diagram). With practice you should become adept at plotting references and the more expert navigators can manage at least two or three a minute when stationary and can also keep up a healthy batting average when the car is moving.

Practise plotting as much as you can and you'll soon speed up — but always take extra care with references like 010101 or 696969. In order to give a really accurate plot (possibly a road beside a grass triangle — beloved by rally organisers) you may be given an eight figure reference, but it is more common for organisers to stick to 'halves' and so a reference will be shown as $100\frac{1}{2}200\frac{1}{2}$ (or, as some purists may prefer, 10052005).

In order to plot references quickly and accurately it is necessary to use a "romer". This is small plastic device, of which there are several makes and which is the navigator's prime tool of his trade. A romer has the scale of the map broken down into tenths and by sliding this along the maps having found the appropriate kilometre square, you can measure off the exact reference accurately and quickly. Romers can carry scales of several maps — possibly 1:50,000, 1:63,360 (the old 1 inch to the mile maps, now replaced in Britain by the 1:50,000 scale) and even 1:126720 scale; this $\frac{1}{2}$ inch to the mile scale is used mostly in Ireland. The scale of 1:50,000 is, of course by far the most popular.

If you are planning to use the romer only with 1:50,000 maps you might round off the other three corners so that you can find the necessary scale instantly, this can save time. The romer should be placed on a loop of string, worn round the neck — there's nothing so elusive as a 'stringless' romer in a bouncing rally car.

Ordnance Survey maps are easlily obtainable and there is an official stockist in practically every town. It is advisable to purchase your maps from one stockist so that you build up a relationship with the retailer; they may then be more helpful when you require maps quickly which are out of stock.

Although British Ordnance Survey maps are the clearest and carry most detail and are possibly the best maps in the world, they do require additional information to be added for rally use. Extra markings (shown in the illustration) should be added in waterproof ink — care must be taken to avoid obliterating information already on the map. Marking should be kept as simple as possible. Many of the top road rally navigators favour markings in yellow or orange felt tip; these will not obliterate anything yet will stand out clearly.

On the latest Ordnance Survey maps (second series 1:50,000) the 'eastings' and 'northings' are marked at intervals across the maps which makes for quicker plotting. You may wish to add a few more of your own as well.

A road which is shown in white on the map may be passable or it may be unsurfaced and peter out into a bog or chassis-breaking impasse. In rally parlance these roads are 'goers' or 'non-goers' and as time progresses the rally navigator will gain more information about these; this information should be added to the map. We recommend a simple line alongside the road or an 'X' to indicate goers and non-goers respectively.

Hump-backed bridges, difficult junctions, 'Give Way' junctions, grass triangles, fords, bad bends, known mud patches, etc., can all be added and built up from information gathered through experience (often bitter) or from reading rally reports in newspapers and magazines.

When you learn something new on a rally, mark it on the map you are using in pencil, then later mark it permanently. You should remember that a broken line along a road does not refer to the standard of road but tells you that the road has no fence or wall.

Mark the number of adjoining maps on each map edge and if you know any particularly tricky section where junctions and tracks hover between the edges of maps, 'doctor' the maps by drawing on the details. You may wish to tape on a section from an adjoining map (you'll find your old maps come in useful for this). Maps can quickly wear at the folds, so a piece of Sellotape stuck on the backs of the corner folds can help to preserve the maps and avoid your trying to navigate your driver through holes!

Make sure you know how to read a map and if you are about to venture onto new territory, have a good look at the map to familiarise yourself with the layout of the land. You should know all the symbols used on the maps; if not, study the key.

Pay attention to the classification of roads and also the various lines used for electricity grids, pipelines and boundaries; these can easily be mixed up. Churches, Youth Hostels, telephone kiosks, milestones and bridges are all good landmarks and help to keep you on route during a rally. When studying new country, pay close attention to contour lines to get some idea of how hilly the country is: the heights of contours are written in the contour lines at intervals along their length. On Ordnance Survey maps they are printed so that they read facing uphill which provides a quick check as to the direction of the slope. Contours close together mean steep slopes and contours further apart mean more gentle ones.

To put the route of a rally on the map you should use a soft pencil (2B or 3B); never have a very sharp point as this may be difficult to erase. Always carry a lot of pencils — they keep breaking and have a habit of jumping out of your fingers and sliding under the seat at the most crucial moments. A small 'spring clip' pencil holder fixed to the dashboard or rear of the sunvisor is a good way of storing spare pencils.

Keep markings simple and never rub fingers over the map as the pencil lead quickly becomes ingrained and makes the map less clear for future occasions.

It is usually best to draw a circle for a control and indicate your route by a line alongside the road with the odd arrow to remind you of your direction of travel.

Road rallies have Competitive, Non-competitive and, sometimes, Special Time Recovery sections, so you will probably wish to use different markings for different sections. *Motoring News* Champion navigator Nigel Harris favours solid pencil lines on both sides of the road on competitive sections while *single* lines on the left of the road indicate non-competitive sections, showing the direction of travel.

There are no fixed rules, so please yourself — but keep it simple.

'Give-way' junctions, noise zones, no-lateness sections, non-competitive sections (where you must *not* make up time) must all be marked clearly. Mark where you change from one map to the other by writing in the margin "CM to ... " with the number of the map you are moving onto.

Although you'll have time cards, roadbooks, regulations and so on in the car, the map is your *working document* and as much information as possible must be kept on it.

RALLY NAVIGATION

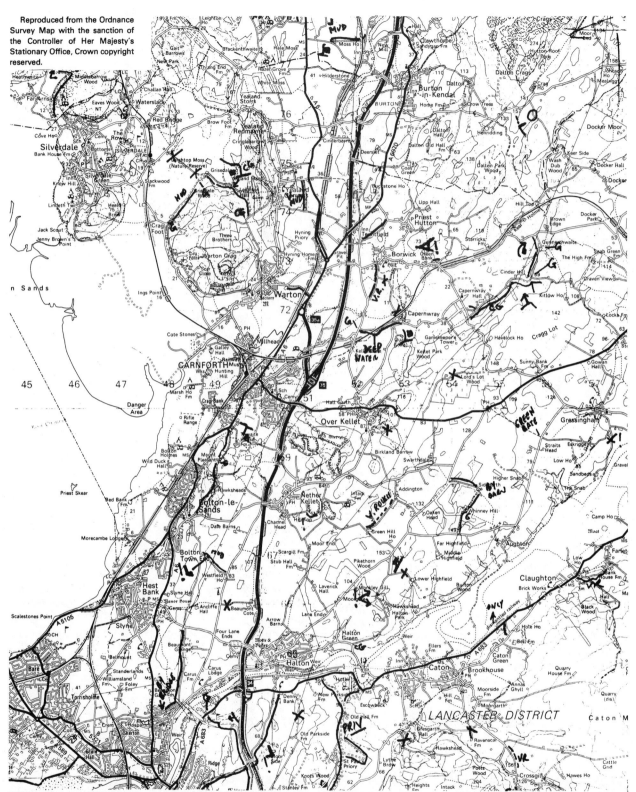

Most navigators add markings to their maps. Eastings and northings are now thoughtfully provided by the Ordnance Survey at 10km intervals to make reference plotting easier. A 'goer' in the case of a white road is marked by a simple line alongside, or may be coloured in yellow or orange by the navigator. A 'non-goer' will have a simple "X" across the road, taking care not to obscure any important printing. Special features marked are an obscure triangle at 538729 (much loved by organisers), a bad bend at 557760 (much worse than the map indicates) and an obscure entrance at 493616. "G" means gate and "CG" cattlegrid. Most other titbits of information are self-explanatory. Budding navigators might care to note that this example of map marking on sheet 97 is purely for demonstration purposes.

62

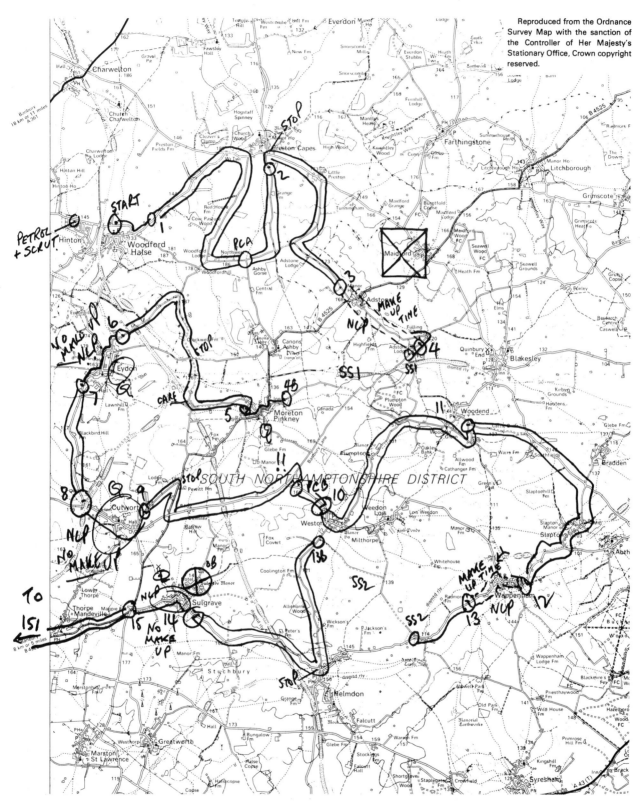

The route should be marked on the map as clearly as possible, in soft pencil. Arrows and lines must not obscure any bends or roads to be used. Note how clearly 'Out of Bounds' areas are marked, as are 'Quiet Areas', 'Stop' junctions and 'No Lateness Penalty' sections. Note that extra comments have been taken from the roadbook and added by the navigator, e.g. "Care", "Make up time" and direction of approach after a triangle which might easily be missed. Special Stage starts and finishes are marked clearly but no markings are shown on the stage in accordance with RACMSA regulations. This route is given purely as an example of how you might like to mark your map – it is not an actual rally.

An illuminated map magnifier is necessary for road rally navigators. This one is made in strong PVC and carries a powerful lens and bulb. For British use a Romer baseplate is incorporated.

Always use a cardboard map board – never, never use metal, wood or anything hard, an accident can have very painful consequences if an unyielding board is rammed into your pelvis. The cardboard should be approximately 18 inches square and is purely used to hold all the maps in position. Some people clip them in position – others let them lie loose. A map board with rally information marked on it is helpful – information like average speeds, maximum and minimum times allowed etc. (one will be penalised for completing some sections in less than three-quarters of the official time). The equations for working out average speeds, lengths of sections etc are also useful.

A simple clipboard should be used as well with important rally documents like route and time cards etc., fixed to it. It is better to have time cards tightly clipped in position – marshals prefer something hard to rest on when signing your card. Incidentally, it is advisable to work out a routine for marshals; you may prefer to open the door and let them lean in. You can shine the light on the board for them and all of this saves time for you. A special light fixed above the passenger door is also very sensible and favoured by the best road navigators (the navigator will control this by a switch in the car).

Always do your utmost to keep your time cards and other documents dry; a ball point will not write on wet, soggy card and a felt-tip will make an unholy mess.

Occasionally on rallies you will be given small route check cards and these should be kept in a pouch or special secure envelope as it can be heartbreaking to discover the loss of a card when you have completed a two-hundred mile rally.

A map measurer (called an opisometer, consisting of a small wheel and dial) is useful to carry, and a pocket calculator (for calculating times and average speeds) should be carried, ideally one with a built-in stop watch. Navigators should keep a close watch on silicone chip technology (not Harry Ramsden's, electronics) because the dramatic advances in the last few years seem likely to continue and are making things easier for navigators.

Probably the most popular device for British navigators is the *Terra Trip* which is equipped with L.E.D. readout in red. The German *Combi Counter* carries a rheostat so that the brightness of the figures can be altered. One model of *Terra Trip* will give you your average speed which can, of course, be useful on longer road events and international rallies.

Many of the works teams make it possible for the navigator to 'zero' the digital trip meter by means of a foot-operated switch similar to an old fashioned dip switch of the type which the authors well remember from their rallying days in Austin A35s and Sprites!

This foot-operated system has obvious advantages when trip distances are incorporated in the notes which are being read on foggy sections. (More about pace notes later).

It is sometimes thought that the dashboard on the navigator's side of the car should be covered with dials and clocks so that it looks like a scaled down version of Concorde's cockpit. This is not true; like everything else to do with navigation it is better to follow the old adage of "keep things simple".

On a British road rally it is quite possible to succeed without any form of clock on the dashboard – a successful navigator may use his wrist watch (also a hand-held stop-watch if there are any sections timed to the second) as well as just a navigator's light and a map magnifier.

Every rally car should really have a flexible navigator's light fitted. There are numerous makes and there are different lengths to choose from. Select one that will suit your car and will reach across the map, which will be on your knee. Some people mount the lights on the gearbox housing or on the door, although this may be a bad thing as the light can easily be knocked off.

The flexible light is used mostly for map work when the car is stationary but if it has to be used when the car is mobile use one with an adjustable shade over the bulb so that it doesn't dazzle the driver. Always carry a spare bulb. Some flexible lights are made with two levels of lighting – a white light for stationary map work and a red one for pace note use.

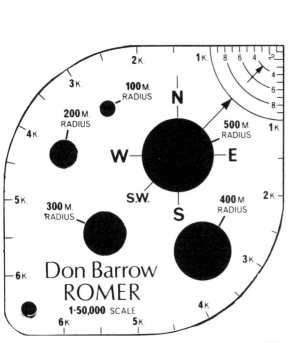

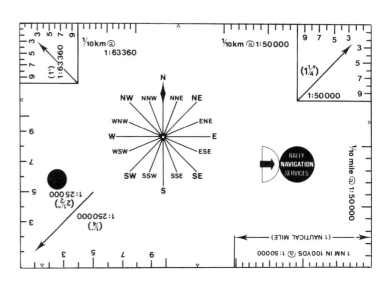

The Romer is the navigator's most important tool of his trade. There are several types. The Don Barrow model carries holes of different diameter for marking noise areas. Rally Navigation Services' model can be used with maps of different scales.

(1) 'Terratrip A.R.C.' This model features two distance displays, time of day and stopwatch. Time displays can be switched to show average speeds and can be calibrated for miles/kilometres/tyre sizes by the use of numbered rotary controls at bottom right-hand corner. The instrument features Liquid Crystal Displays (LCD) which are internally illuminated.

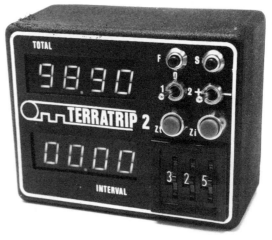

(2) 'Terratrip 2' A less expensive and simpler instrument performing most of the above functions and entirely suitable for all but the top professional co-driver. This is available with LCD displays or with bright red Lighting Emitting Diode (LED) figures. Distance displays can be calibrated. There are other Terratrip models.

The British made Terratrip electronic measuring devices are widely used throughout the world and make life a lot easier for navigators. Don't worry! They're easier to operate than they look and full instructions are supplied.

The co-driver's role as 'office manager' may include responsibility for the "Carnet de Passage en Douanes" – in other words, the document which helps you get spares through Customs. Almost as complicated as an homologation form.

Keep all non-fixed items of equipment stored carefully and always in the same place, say in a door pocket or document case under the dashboard.

Maps, other than the ones you are using, should be kept in sequence and in a handy position. Another useful tip is to take a few notes of surrounding areas as you never know when you may have to go off route in the event of a diversion or retirement (or quite simply through getting lost!).

Some method of magnifying the map is essential. There are illuminated magnifers which work from batteries and while these are useful as spares they are not recommended for full time use as the batteries might run down at a crucial moment.

There *are* navigators still using the old Eolites once used by R.A.F. navigators in World War II but now the most popular is the Don Barrow Light which has a built-in scale base (removable) a rheostat and powerful magnifying lens. Many top road rally crews even carry a complete spare light. Don Barrow, by the way, was several times *Motoring News* Champion Navigator in the Sixties.

If you wear spectacles (many navigators do) remember to keep them in position with a cord at the back of the neck. Always carry a spare pair and consider plastic lenses – they are safer.

Your driver will probably expect you to be the bookworm! You should be the one to send for regulations and you should then study them very carefully. You must know what time you need to report for scrutineering, when and how the route will be given out, how much time you can make up, the difference between stage penalties and road marks, the penalties for lateness, etc. Many of these are very small points, but a mistake with any one of them could wreck your chances on an event.

When you get to the start of a rally the route you are given is obviously of vital importance, and so is any list of black-spots and 'out of bounds' areas which you *must* observe. Drivers are notorious for wandering off aimlessly during the preliminaries to the start of a rally, so find your man a particular job to keep him busy.

On the majority of rallies you will find yourself plotting the route from map references, often with directions of approach and departure stipulated. Sometimes, particularly on smaller events, you may be given the route in more bizarre ways but if the rally is properly run this needn't throw you because no responsible organiser will risk the public nuisance of cars milling about lost because he was too smart in his route instructions.

Most crews incur 'fails' at some time in their career because of wrong directions of approach or departure. Always check these very thoroughly when they are stipulated and remember not to get west and east confused. You might think this is elementary but a great number of experienced competitors very easily confuse south-west with south-east and, needless to say, it is a favourite trick of organisers to place controls at junctions requiring an approach from one of these two directions.

Once you are under way on the event, keep your driver in touch with what is happening, but don't babble on too much; give him a chance to settle down, perhaps calling out the occasional phone box or something clearly visible to help him to build his confidence in you. When you are starting as a navigator, don't try to read every bend on the map to the driver because you will probably find that

RS 4	SUTTON PARK TO BEWDLEY (VIA BANNERS GATE)	DISTANCE	35.47 MILES
page 65 · via PC 4		TIME	0 HRS 59 MINS
		SPEED	36.1 MPH

Ref	MILES INTER	MILES TOTAL	INFORMATION		MAP	ROAD	DIRECTION	Miles to TC
1	–	0.00	FTC4: SUTTON PARK		139			35.47
2	0.41	0.41	LEAVE PARK		139/091955			35.06
3			PC4: BANNERS GATE		CARDS: RS3, SS4.			
4	0.74	1.15	TOP RANK CLUB			GREAT BARR 2		34.32
5	0.41	1.56	ESSO					33.91
6	0.26	1.82	THE TREES			GREAT BARR		33.65
7	0.49	2.31			A4041	GREAT BARR		33.16
8	1.25	3.56	RIGHT HAND LANE PRENDRE DE VOIE DE DROITE SCOTT ARMS & BP		A34	WALSALL		31.91
9	0.39	3.95	SHELL			MOTORWAY M6		31.52

A page from the roadbook of the Lombard-RAC Rally. Both intermediate and cumulative mileage distances are shown. The 'Tulip' method of route instruction is in worldwide use.

	RS 20B	MACHYNLLETH TO PANTPERTHOG	**DISTANCE**	2.78 *MILES*

page **126**	via **PC**		**TIME**	0 *HRS* 8 *MINS*
			SPEED	20.9 *MPH*

Ref	MILES		INFORMATION		MAP	ROAD	DIRECTION	Miles to TC
	INTER	TOTAL						
1		0.00	TC20B: MACHYNLLETH 'OUT'		135/747008			2.78
2	0.05	0.05	CLOCK TOWER			A487 DOLGELLAU		2.73
3	0.75	0.80				A487 DOLGELLAU		1.98
4	0.53	1.33				A487 DOLGELLAU		1.45
5	1.35	2.68	ENTER FOREST		135/748043			0.10
6	0.10	2.78	ATC21: PANTPERTHOG					0.00
7			IDEAL TIME: / ACTUAL TIME: / LATENESS:					
8	0.17	–	SS21: PANTPERTHOG		8.2 MILES, GRAVEL.			
9			MAX TIME: / ACTUAL TIME: / LATENESS:					

Another page from a Lombard-RAC Rally roadbook. Note the spaces provided by the organisers so that competitors can enter their own time details. The 'shaded' sections indicate gravel roads.

TIME	INC	CUM	TULIP	REMARKS
	4.58		↑-	
		22.54		"MILE 236"
	3.60			
		26.14	⊠	RIGHT ONTO DIRT ONTO 567. BEAVERHEAD LODGE.
	.12			SERVICE LOCATION. (UNLEADED ONLY)
		26.26	🕐	
	.05			TRANSIT CONTROL.
(14)		26.31/0.00	START	START STAGE 7, ZERO ODO. LENGTH: 6.77
	1.72			
		1.72		CAUTION! NARROW CATTLE GUARD. MAIN ROAD KEEPS RIGHT.
	1.58			
		3.30		ACUTE LEFT ONTO 58. ROAD NARROWS AND IS ROUGH TO FINISH.
	.68			
		3.98		MAIN ROAD KEEPS LEFT.
	.84			
		4.82	↑!	CAUTION! WATER-BAR
	.08			
		4.90		CATTLE GUARD.

Route instructions American style! Note the detailed explanation of hazards. A water-bar is a point where the road crosses a stream, incidentally. This is a section of Arizona's Coronado Rally.

although you are making a very good job of it, you are actually on the wrong road!

Above all, *concentrate* (that word again!) on making sure that you are on the right road at all times, and that you guide your driver down the correct slots (turnings) without overshooting. When you can do this consistently well, start to call out the bad bends, then with experience you can start to call out more gradual ones; how far you pursue this depends on just what information your driver needs. If he is experienced he'll probably be frightening himself so much that he won't be paying all that much attention to what you are saying anyway.

Marshals are an important part of a rally; always be nice to them. Present your route card to them properly and if you haven't got a light on the roof to help them, hold your map light over your route card. Unless you have a lot of time in hand, don't get too involved in chatting to marshals as you may break your concentration. Try not to shout or argue with marshals as you are seldom likely to win; they have the upper hand! Some people still try to 'shout up' the time or bully marshals into giving them the time they want but most marshals have already been warned of this trick.

Make sure a marshal signs in the right place and *check* his work immediately. His is an arduous job and inevitably human error creeps in — particularly on a long, cold, wet night. Keep your road book clean if you can and if a marshal happens to make a mistake in entering a time or direction of approach then get him to scrub out the original entry completely, re-write the correct entry and initial or sign this alteration — it will be difficult to have things changed later.

Don't let a marshal merely alter a figure as most rally regulations state that "any items on time cards that have been altered or appear to have been tampered with may be deemed not to have been made". You have been warned!

If you can, stay in the car at controls. Check your map work and time cards. Don't be eager to leave the car and blab your times to other competitors; they may be encouraged to try harder and pull back a deficit!

After a stop of any kind, remember to tell your driver what the next section is like — it is *your* fault if he sets off at half throttle when he ought to be pressing on.

We've talked about the importance of time-keeping — let's now mention the types of timing.

On most road rallies the marshals will hold the watches — usually clear, accurate, waterproof clocks or digital timepieces. Marshals will read off the time in hours and minutes, always reading to the previous minute e.g., 06 hour 37 mins 59 secs will read 06.37. On some competitive sections or on special tie-deciding parts seconds may be used and the full time written in.

Where organisers use watches with hands (i.e. non-digital types) at controls where times are to be recorded to the second, the navigator should be wary of the most competent marshal giving a 'wrong minute'. For example, 22hrs 15min 58sec is easily mis-read as 22.16.58 because the minute hand is virtually on the sixteen.

A marshal's timepiece will either be set to the time of day, or more likely to "Targa Time". This takes its name from the rally that first adopted this timing — Oxford University's Targa Rusticana, one of the classic road rallies of the sixties. It's a very clever but simple idea. The clock at the start of the rally is set so that car number 1 will depart at 00.01, car number 2 at 00.02 and so on. Car number 61 will depart at 01.01. The timepiece at each subsequent control is set back by the amount of time allocated to the section. Therefore, if car number 1 is on time at every control he'll clock in at 00.01 everywhere. It's easy for marshals to operate (less likelihood of a mistake) and easy for results teams.

Organisers will set and seal all timepieces prior to the rally. These will be hired from companies who specialise in hiring out timekeeping equipment to motor clubs.

At one time competitors carried the watches used to record their progress but today only the smallest club rally provides competitors with 'sealed watches'. These are set back from BBC time by their competition number so making them all due at each control at the time shown on the routecard. This system of timekeeping is open to abuse by competitors and marshals so is now never used on better events.

Stage rallies are always timed at normal time of day and the stages themselves are timed to the second or even fraction of a second. Generally speaking, the bigger the rally the better the timepieces but all should be set by competent registered timekeepers. Printing clocks are also used occasionally.

At the end of a special stage a marshal will signal or phone through the precise moment that each car crosses the flying finish line to another marshal holding the watch at the stop line; cars stop at this marshal to have times recorded. The watch is sometimes kept at the 'flying finish' line and the time radioed to the stop line, but an organiser is better advised to adopt the former method in case there are any mis-read times and navigators ask to see the watch.

When you move on to International events, the navigator becomes very much an office manager. You will need maps of course — quarter inch maps in the UK are close to the Michelins you will use on the Continent and will give you a feel for the scale — but there will be a lot more than maps to think about!

SOUTH BARRULE.   11

50 °%/C→ Lg FR⊕

70 FR÷ + FL 100

/C + FL NARROWS 70

R̈ + L @ WALL → ⤒ TURN HPR

50 /C KeepR + L̈ → VFL

150 L↘

TRANSLATION.

50 YDS ABSOLUTE OVER CREST INTO

LONG FAST RIGHT PLUS   70 YDS

FAST RIGHT MINUS AND FAST LEFT 100 YDS.

CREST + FAST LEFT NARROWS   70 YDS

ABSOLUTE RIGHT AND ABSOLUTE LEFT AT WALL INTO

SIGN TURN HAIRPIN RIGHT 50 YDS.

CREST KEEP RIGHT AND ABSOLUTE LEFT INTO

VERY FAST LEFT   150 YDS

Pacenotes are essential for a good performance on a non-secret route. These 'South Barrule' notes were prepared by Jimmy McRae and Ian Grindrod for a Manx International Rally which they won. On the right we show how they would be read to the driver. When writing notes, try to avoid starting successive lines with the same symbol or word – this prevents the wrong line being read.

Incidentally, drivers are a neurotic breed and can quite easily overcomplicate things so remember to try and keep things basic – there are, we notice, phrases consisting of four words used here to describe one type of bend which could take some understanding.

41
/ 1980   STAGES 41 + 44 + 47   1/6

START reverse △ on L   SINTRA
                              10.5 k

50 R + long L ? 50 ! >R

50 Ulong R 100 FL 50

L̊ 30 FR 30 ER? 50

long L > 50 ER 30 EL? +

ER? FR/B + long FL? 70

long KL + EL VUlong R >

TRANSLATION

50 RIGHT AND LONG LEFT—MAYBE 50
CAUTION TIGHTENS RIGHT 50 VERY LONG
RIGHT 100 FLAT LEFT 50 ABSOLUTE
LEFT 30 FLAT RIGHT 30 EASY RIGHT—
MAYBE 50 LONG LEFT TIGHTENS 50 EASY
RIGHT 30 EASY LEFT—MAYBE AND
EASY RIGHT—MAYBE FLAT RIGHT OVER
BROW AND LONG FLAT LEFT—MAYBE
70 LONG K LEFT AND EASY LEFT
VERY, VERY LONG RIGHT TIGHTENS

And another example of pacenotes. These were used by Ari Vatanen and David Richards on the Portugal Rally. Notice how the notes of different crews bear little similarity to each other.

Flat out over crest ...even clubmen find pace notes essential on some events! This is Ron Davies and Peter Vallis on the Manx National.

You will have to arrange insurance, hotels, passports, visas (if any), boat tickets, Carnets, maybe airline tickets, etc, etc, etc! And by the way, you will need a "Foreign Event Visa" from the R.A.C, which allows you to take part in overseas events – this only costs a few pounds and includes the basic medical insurance.

Then you may have to organise fuel arrangements, service points – where and when brake pads should be renewed and so on. You will probably be in charge of planning service.

Realise that overseas events are not run on the same lines as British events – so don't assume domestic custom and practice necessarily applies – and it is important that you study the regulations carefully and make sure that you know what you can and cannot do without penalty. Ask the organisers and the more experienced competitors if you have any doubts whatsoever.

Be particularly careful about booking in at controls as many people have incurred 'early penalty' marks because they didn't study the regulations properly.

Don't forget to make sure you have all the necessary inoculations for the countries you are visiting (making sure you have them in good time and have left the required space of time between injections). Don't become a sort of travelling Boots, but do take along the odd tablet for stomach upsets, diarrhoea, headaches and sunstroke; your doctor will advise you.

On most stage events and nearly all Internationals you will encounter 'Tulip arrows' because they are by far the simplest way of indicating a route. Tulip arrows are so-called because they were first used on the Dutch Tulip Rally many years ago – not because some of the diagrams look like tulips. Unless you have absolute faith in the organisers, plot a Tulip route on the maps then put the map numbers in the road book (the R.A.C. Rally does this for you), then even if you just use the road book you will be able to dig out the appropriate map if you hit problems.

If you make route or navigational notes Tulip arrows are by far the best way because you can easily and diagrammatically portray each junction. If you are contemplating doing a winter event, remember that snow might cover milestones and road markings, so only record items which will stand proud.

Pace notes play a prominent part in many International events and although you'll be well advised to steer clear of them in the earlier stages of your career you'll find them a necessary part of your life later on. Making pace notes and all forms of recceing is regarded by many as boring, futile and a complete waste of time. It's certainly very time and petrol-consuming but if other crews are using notes, you'll have to do likewise to stay competitive.

Pace notes are a way by which the co-driver can remind or tell the driver about the road they are approaching. Ideally the notes should be made by

ON. 1

TC2 OLEPOLOS — TC3 NAROK

135.4 KMS.   ALL DIRT EXCEPT 8 KMS. FAST TAR.
              MANY ROUGH PATCHS.   1 PASSAGE CONTROL.

TIME ALLOWED : 70 MINS.   EXPECT 10 MINS LATE
ROLLE TIME : 110 MINS.

DEP. TC2	16	47
TIME ALLOWED	1	10
ARR. TC3	17	57

0.00   TURN R AT   TC2

KR   EL/C — ROUGH 50   ROUGH ER

100   NARROW BRIDGE & HUMP   100

BUMPY — KR/BRIDGE & CARE STOP — BAD HOLE

EL — ER   ER & BIG BUMP   200   KR   EL

ROUGH KR — EL   VERY ROUGH KL   100

CARE C — DRIFT   200 ~ WATCH ROCKS IN ROAD

ER — EL   300   CARE , V. SLOW — RIVER CROSSING &

KEEP R AT EXIT — R   200   ROAD NOW BETTER BUT

WATCH   FOR   ANIMALS   CROSSING

Pace notes for long distance events take the form of route instructions and carry many descriptive passages. Note 'tourist guide' references to animals and rivers on this page of Safari notes. The panel of times is redrawn from the official roadbook and the co-driver's own comments about lateness added.

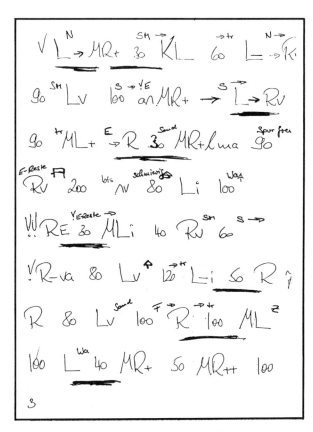

Although we don't profess to understand every word, you might wish to study Walter Röhrl's example of ice notes in German for the Monte Carlo Rally which he won. Added comments are made by ice-note crews prior to the stage closing for non-rally traffic. These would be in coloured pen, of course.

the crews themselves although it may be necessary to use notes made by other members of a team on occasions. This can be dangerous and there have been expensive accidents as a result of the mis-interpretation of instructions perhaps because the terminology used by one crew differed from that used by another.

If pace notes have been made properly (preferably by several runs over a stage) they can be both fast and safe. Pace notes can be a great help to performance on a stage because they present a picture to the driver of the road which he cannot fully see; they help the driver to keep up the speed of the car and he should be able to position the car properly at all times.

If possible, pace notes should be finally checked at rally speeds, preferably in a rally car (initial note-making can be done in a much slower vehicle, say a hire car).

Brian Culcheth, whose career as a top driver spanned two decades, has run schools to teach people the art of pace note making. He claims that ninety per cent of his pupils fail to relate pace notes to gears. In other words, a driver dictating notes should relate them to the gear in which he will be travelling on the rally; this will keep his terminology constant.

A driver will dictate notes as he drives over a road to be used on the rally, giving the navigator the information he wants to hear later. The navigator will write the notes in pencil (which for some reason is easier to control) in large-style printing with only a few lines to a page and large line spaces.

Pocket tape recorders are not really a good idea – you may put in too much detail and if they decide not to operate at a crucial moment you will have nothing to copy out. Put in various geographic notes (but not too many) as you will be able to keep

STAGE TIME RECORDS

Competitor Number									
Driver									
Brought Forward									
Stage No.									
Stage No.									
Stage No.									
Stage No.									
Stage No.									
Stage No.									
Stage No.									
Stage No.									
Stage No.									
Stage No.									
Stage No.									
Stage No.									
Stage No.									
Stage No.									
Stage No.									
Stage No.									

All co-drivers should keep a close eye on their rivals' times at every stage and will use a chart of similar design to this to record all the times. They'll probably obtain the times from the competitors themselves or from team personnel and will always verify the times on official bulletins.

ITINÉRAIRE: LONDRES - GB

Contrôles horaires et de passage	Distances partielles	Distances totales
LONDRES	0	0
Douvres (CP)		
CALAIS	119	119
Le Choléra (CP)		
REIMS	310	429
Stenay (CP)		
LANGRES	317	746
Conliège (CP)		
MOIRANS-EN-MONTAGNE	200	946
Ambérieu-en-Bugey (CP)		
Seyssel (CP)		
AIX LES BAINS	173	1119
Bourget-du-Lac (CP)		
VOREPPE	106	1225
GRENOBLE	21	1246

Cartes Michelin utilisées pour le parcours en France:
Nº 53 - 56 - 57 - 62 - 66 - 70 - 74.

Monte Carlo Rally organisers give route details in their regulations. This page shows the route for London starters. Note the Michelin map numbers which are stated.

Communes	Routes	Distances partielles	Distances totales
Vendredi 28 Janvier 1983			
35ème Secteur: BIF D 2211 / D 5 (CP) - (ST AUBAN) - LODA: 97,40 km - Temps idéal: 1 h 56			
28ème **BIF D 2211 / D 5**	D 5		
Épreuve **BIF D 5 / D 10**	D 5		
Chronométrée **LES 4 CHEMINS**	D 2	16,00	16,00
16 km environ Gréolières	D 2	10,00	26,00
Coursegoules	D 2	11,00	37,00
Bouyon	D 1	12,00	49,00
Le Broc	D 1	8,00	57,00
Carros	D 1	3,00	60,00
C.P. Bif D 1 / D 2209	D 2209	1,30	61,30
Bif D 2209 / N 202	N 202	10,60	71,90
Alpes-Maritimes Plan du Var			
Bif N 202 / D 2565			
(Pont Durandy)	D 2565	2,00	74,50
St Jean la Rivière	D 2565	10,00	84,70
Lantosque			
Bif D 2565 / D 73	D 73	8,90	93,10
LODA	D 73	4,50	97,40

Communes	Routes	Distances partielles	Distances totales
Vendredi 28 Janvier 1983			
36ème Secteur: LODA (PEILLE) - (BIF N 7 / V 9) MONACO: 60,50 km Temps idéal: 1 h 15			
29ème **LODA**	D73		
Épreuve **COL DE PORTE**			
Chronométrée **COL ST ROCH**			
16 km environ **BIF D 73 / D 2565**	D 2566		
LUCERAM	D 2566	16,50	
L'Escarène			
Bif D 2566 / D 2204	D 2204	6,80	23,30
Bif D 2204 / D 21	D 21	0,30	23,60
La Grave de Peille			
Bif D 21 / D 53	D 53	7,00	30,60
C.P. Peille		6,00	36,60
La Turbie	D 53	9,30	45,90
Bif D 53 / D 2564	D 2564	0,50	46,40
Bif D 2564 / D 51	D 51	4,80	51,20
Bif D 51 / N 7	N 7	1,90	53,20
C.P. Bif N 7 / V 9	N 7	1,90	55,00
Bif N 7 / N 559	N 559	0,80	55,80
MONACO			
(Route de la Piscine)		4,70	60,50

Here are the more detailed instructions for the final night of the event in the French Alps.

4. Controls will be as follows:

   (a) Time Control (TC): at the beginning and end of each Road Section.

   (b) At Rest Halts there will be two Time Controls: a TC 'In' for arriving competitors and a TC 'Out' for departing competitors. The start of the Rally will be regarded as a TC 'Out' and the finish will be regarded as a TC 'In'.

   (c) Passage Control (PC): situated at appropriate places for ensuring that a competitor is following the correct route.

   (d) Special Control (SC): situated at some point within 500 metres after a Secret Check.

   (e) Special Stage Start Control (SSS): the start line for a Special Stage.

   (f) Special Stage Finish Control (SSF): situated approximately 200 metres after the finish line for a Special Stage, the finish line being crossed non-stop.

5. It is forbidden under pain of exclusion:

   (a) To enter a Control Area in any direction other than that of the Rally Route.

   (b) To re-cross or re-enter a control area once checking-in has taken place at this control.

6. A Secret Check may be located at any point on the route for the purpose of checking that competitors are following the official route, are complying with any specific directions given in the Road Book, and are not travelling at an excessive speed or causing excessive noise.

   If possible competitors will be informed of any alleged infringement at a Special Control situated after a Secret Check.

7. Times will be recorded in Time of Day using the 24 hour system as follows:

   (a) in hours and minutes at each TC, SSS and SC. (In this case the recording will be to the preceding whole minute e.g. 13 hr. 18 min. 59 secs. will be recorded as 13 hr. 18 min.).

   (b) in hours, minutes and seconds at each SSF. (In this case the recording will be to the preceding whole second).

   (c) Competitors will be given the opportunity to examine the clock at points where time is recorded and it is the competitors responsibility to ensure that times are correctly recorded on the Time Cards.

   (d) A competitor who interferes with an Official Clock, whether accidentally or otherwise, may be penalised by a time penalty or by exclusion.

8. No time will be recorded at a Passage Control, the stamp or signature of the Officials providing proof of a competitor reporting there.

9. Controls will open 15 minutes before the Schedule Time of the first competitor. Special Stages will open at the Schedule Time of the first

28

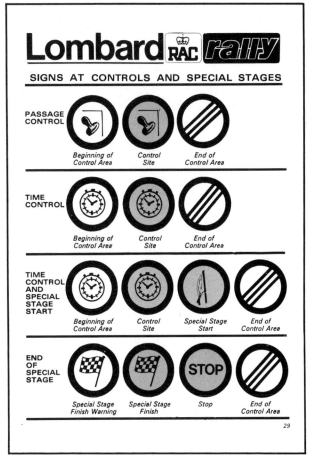

Lombard RAC rally

SIGNS AT CONTROLS AND SPECIAL STAGES

PASSAGE CONTROL
Beginning of Control Area   Control Site   End of Control Area

TIME CONTROL
Beginning of Control Area   Control Site   End of Control Area

TIME CONTROL AND SPECIAL STAGE START
Beginning of Control Area   Control Site   Special Stage Start   End of Control Area

END OF SPECIAL STAGE
Special Stage Finish Warning   Special Stage Finish   Stop   End of Control Area

29

Two pages from the regulations for the Lombard-RAC Rally. Note the self-explanatory international symbols for controls, etc. ('Shaded' signs are red, the rest yellow).

CONCURRENT / ENTRANT / BEWERBER
NOM / SURNAME / NAME   PRENOM / CHRISTIAN NAME / VORNAME

M. Mme Mlle
Mr Mrs Miss
H. Fr. Frl.

PSEUDONYME EVENTUEL / PSEUDONYM / RUFNAME   NATIONALITE / NATIONALITY / STAATSANGEHORIGKEIT

Adresse:

Numéro de Licence   délivrée par:

1er CONDUCTEUR / 1st DRIVER / 1. FAHRER
NOM / SURNAME / NAME   PRENOM / CHRISTIAN NAME / VORNAME

M. Mme Mlle
Mr Mrs Miss
H. Fr. Frl.

PSEUDONYME EVENTUEL / PSEUDONYM / RUFNAME   NATIONALITÉ / NATIONALITY / STAATSANGEHORIGKEIT

Adresse:
    Téléphone:

Numéro de Licence   délivrée par

COÉQUIPIER / TEAM MATE / BEIFAHRER
NOM / SURNAME / NAME   PRENOM / CHRISTIAN NAME / VORNAME

M. Mme Mlle
Mr Mrs Miss
H. Fr. Frl.

PSEUDONYME EVENTUEL / PSEUDONYM / RUFNAME   NATIONALITE / NATIONALITY / STAATSANGEHORIGKEIT

Adresse:
    Téléphone:

Numéro de Licence   délivrée par

VILLE DE DÉPART / TOWN OF DEPARTURE / STARTORT:

Je souhaite participer au Classement "PROMOTION" (cf. Art. 5b)
I wish to take part in the Classification "PROMOTION" (cf. Art. 5b)
Ich wunsche in der Klassement "PROMOTION" teilnehmen (cf. Art. 5b)

FICHE DE RENSEIGNEMENTS - INFORMATION FORM - AUSKUNFTSFORMULAR

Marque de la voiture
Make of the car   Type   Année
Fabrikat des Fahrzeuges

N° Châssis
Chassis number   N° Moteur
Fahrgestell Nr   Engine number
    Motor Nr

N° Immatriculation
Registration number
Pol. Kennzeichen

Carrosserie: Type
Coachwork: Type   Nombre de places   Couleur
Bauart: Type   Number of seats   Colour
    Anzahl der Sitzplatze   Farbe

Nombre de cylindres / Number of cylinders / Anzahl der Zylinder	Course / Stroke / Hub	Alésage d'origine / Original Bore / Original Bohrung	Alésage réel / Real Bore / Wirkliche Bohrung	Cylindrée d'origine / Original Cylinder capacity / Original Hubraum	Cylindrée réelle / Real Cylinder capacity / Wirklicher Hubraum

Modifications apportées / Modifications brought / Vorgenommenen Anderungen

RENSEIGNEMENT OBLIGATOIRE   FICHE D'HOMOLOGATION FIA / FISA N°
    RECOGNITION FIA / FISA N°

J'engage ma voiture dans le **groupe**   et la **classe**
I am entering my car in the **group**   and the **class**
Ich melde mein Fahrzeuge für die **gruppe**   und die Klasse
conformément à l'annexe J au Code Sportif International.
    Certifié exact   Certified exact   Wahrheitsgetreu bestätigt

Signature du Concurrent: **Signature of the Competitor:**   **Unterschrift des Bewerbers:**

An entry form for the Monte Carlo Rally.

Co-drivers rarely hit the headlines but Arne Hertz has been at the top of his profession for more years than most.

your place better. Mention the odd signpost, house or sign, and keep your notes in a spiral bound book, written in black so that they can be photocopied and pages interchanged if necessary.

When re-checking the notes (remember, most crews will have as many runs over a stage as they possibly can) all modifications are also made in pencil and when the crew is satisfied that the notes are correct the navigator will write *over* them in a black felt-tip pen. All the background pencil markings and alterations can be removed with a soft eraser.

It is not a good idea to write out notes in rough and re-copy them neatly later; even the most proficient navigator runs the risk of missing out a symbol or even a line when re-writing, and if he doesn't have a chance to re-check the finished notes on the road itself he could be in big trouble on the actual rally.

The language used in pace notes must be clear and fully understood between driver and navigator. There is no standard language and many top crews have a system which is unique to them. Some people talk about bends in degrees (careful that degrees and speeds don't become confused), others

talk about flat bends, easy bends, crests, etc. Avoid the use of words like 'slight' which could be confused with 'right'. 'K' is often used as this has a clear, unconfused sound but means the same thing as slight — derived from the idea that you are going up the arm of the 'K' (probably in second gear).

Speaking of language, it is interesting to note that English is the most widely used system in notes. Even Hannu Mikkola of Finland and his Swedish co-driver Arne Hertz use English notes rather than their native tongues.

A further sophistication of pace notes are ice notes which may be used on snowy and icy stages. Just prior to the passage of the rally an experienced crew will pass over the stage, marking patches of ice and snow on copies of the notes — probably by underlining sections in red. These will then be passed to the team cars before they do the stage. The ice crews may also recommend the pattern of tyres to be used.

Lest all this talk of pace notes should confuse the beginner, let us remind one and all that pace notes are only used at a fairly advanced stage of rallying and only over roads where practising is allowed.

Any form of practice is strictly forbidden on a British forest rally and even the Lombard R.A.C. Rally bans practice — the only event in the World Championship to do so.

Under R.A.C. regulations you are not allowed to have anything relating to a stage (other than the start and finish) marked on a map. It is, therefore, very difficult to follow the stage, even though most of the forest tracks can be seen on the O.S. map. All a navigator can do is look out for arrows and work out where the stage is going from the direction in which they point.

The only way to know a stage route beforehand is by experience; most British forest stages feature the same route on every event and as a navigator is given the length of the stage he can probably work out where the route will go. None of this, of course, is much help other than to warn drivers of noted hazards. If you try to 'read' a forest track to a driver as you might a stage on a road rally you will find there is no benefit and you will almost certainly slow him down.

Of course, if you follow the course through a forest on the map, in the event of a breakdown (or crash) you will at least know where you are. As navigator, it will be your job to walk for help (of course) and it is useful to spot that the stage finish is just a hundred yards away through the trees rather than following the arrows round the stage for ten miles!

9 A rally diary

You might be forgiven for thinking that in order to take part successfully in a rally you have only three steps to take:

1) *Submit the entry to the organisers.*
2) *Prepare the car.*
3) *Get yourselves to the start by the appointed hour.*

These three things must all be done, of course, but there are many more steps to be taken before, during and after an event before you can say everything is under control.

The purpose of this chapter is to try to place the more important steps in order so that you can see the areas to which you should devote attention at various times. Professional teams have — or should have — every item organised down to the last detail with comprehensive books of crew movements, timetables and schedules. This ensures that everything runs smoothly and avoids last minute panics.

A crew that arrives at the start within minutes of their starting time, or one which has spent half the previous night on the telephone trying to locate an elusive service crew, or one that has had a last minute panic to finds maps or tyres, is just not going to perform as well on an event as a well-organised crew. So ... get organised!

If the co-driver is doing his job properly, much of his duties will have been completed well before the start of the rally. In the case of private entries the driver will probably help in a lot of the pre-rally activities but for the purpose of this chapter let us assume that our co-driver is taking charge of *all* arrangements; we shall therefore address the reader in the role of co-driver. And although you will probably start on short events, near to where you live, we have covered a more elaborate event because the problems are greater.

So, let us suppose that you are planning to enter a one-day stage rally in Britain some 150 miles from home. These are some of the steps you should take prior to the event. We have shown them in a diary form for ease of reference. Many of the suggested timings are approximate and you may disagree with them; there are no hard and fast rules.

Incidentally, as a driver or co-driver, it is advisable to make some sort of planned competition programme for a full year (this helps budgeting) and try to adhere to it as far as possible. Decide if you are going to tackle any local or major championships. Decide who does what before each event, so that you do not arrive in a town at midnight to find that you have no beds because each thought the other had made the bookings.

All of the following timings are calculated from the day of the rally.

Two months prior:
Write for regulations — organisers addresses are usually shown in the motoring press. Study the regulations and ensure that the car is suitable for the event (in terms of preparation and homologation). Be sure that the crew has (or can obtain) suitable grades of competition licence.

As soon as possible after receiving the regulations:
Submit entry forms to organisers together with team entry form and service crew request forms (if applicable). Send the appropriate fee, preferably by cheque.

Study the regulations to find the location of start, half way and finish, and decide how many (if any) hotel rooms you will require. Many rally organisers specify the hotel to be used as rally headquarters and often list other suitable hotels. Some even list hotel room rates and might include official booking forms with the regulations. It is quite common for organisers to negotiate special rates with hoteliers.

It helps the efficiency of a team if all personnel are housed at a convenient place prior to the rally. The most suitable hotels fill quickly — book early.

By the way, if all this sounds a bit grandiose and expensive, well, nobody should kid themselves that motor sport is cheap. However if the cost of hotels frightens you, try bed and breakfast places — or perhaps a caravan or tent.

If possible avoid driving a long way just before the start of a rally — you may save a lodging bill but you may not perform at 100% efficiency because of fatigue.

Try to discover from the regulations the types of stages and whether any practice is necessary or allowed (for the purpose of this exercise we will assume that there is no practice, therefore your entourage will travel to the rally just one day before the start). The organisers will probably advise you of stage surfaces; if there is any doubt from the regulations telephone the organisers who may give you a little more information without actually revealing details of the route.

Discuss with your driver the mechanical and tyre requirements. Ensure that tyres of the right type are ordered. Have enough spare wheels.

Make sure that any parts needed for the car are available or ordered in good time and work out a car preparation programme. Some things are going to need replacing at given intervals — it makes sense to order them well in advance.

Sort out a service crew, though *only* if one is allowed. Make a detailed check list of the parts and tools they must carry — works service crews have detailed lists of everything down to the last washer. Allow time for proper maintenance work to be carried out on the service car itself — it often gets forgotten.

Order Ordnance Survey maps for yourself and the service crew, as well as $\frac{1}{4}$ inch maps or other small scale road maps for the service crew who will not need detailed maps for the whole route (petrol company maps are often quite adequate, and so is the Haynes Motoring Atlas)

One or two weeks prior:
Receive final regulations from organisers. These will spell out any extra requirements. Possibly additional maps, scrutineers' requirements and more details about the rally will be given in the final regulations. Some route details and instructions about timing, arrowing and service crew arrangements will be given.

Above all, the final regulations will tell you where to start, when to start and what time and where you must report for scrutineering. An entry list will be included and you will see the number allocated to your car. You will probably be given individual reporting times for scrutineering. Incidentally, if you don't like your starting number there is very little you can do about it. *Don't* ring the organisers bewailing the fact that your position is too low in the list and that you ought to be ahead of Fred Bloggs as you beat him in the last event. The organisers will be far too busy to listen to your twittering.

The driver must be told of any changes notified in the final regulations. Many people get caught out with things that have not been done through not noting changes. Fire extinguisher requirements, the permanent fixing of tip-forward driving seats, fire-proofing, spotlights, etc. are often mentioned in this context.

Let your driver know the salient details of the rally. Let him know the time that you and the service crew must leave home, and the time that it will take to get to the start. Distances of the rally etc. are also important. Don't fill his head with too much or else he will forget the more important points. If you haven't received confirmation of hotel bookings, check with the hotel that all is in order. There is nothing like a rally for throwing hotel reservation desks into chaos.

Make sure that the car is beginning to look as though it will make the start line. Make sure that any parts which were expected to arrive have been delivered. If not, go for them. Do not rely on British Rail or the post.

As soon as possible, your driver should be testing the car. He should be making sure that everything is to his liking. On the way to the start cover a few miles briskly on a quiet road just finally to shake-down you and the car.

Day prior:
Arrive in good time for scrutineering. Rally scrutineers sometimes tuck themselves away in back street garages which may be difficult to find. Make sure that the crash helmets are with the car for scrutineering (not in your hotel bedroom). Check if you have to report to Rally Headquarters within a specified time after leaving scrutineering. If so, keep an eye on this as you can be penalised for being late.

Go with your driver to signing on. Take your competititon licences (and Entrant's licence if necessary) and anything else that final regulations ask you to show (possibly club membership cards or insurance certificates).

Collect road books, time cards or whatever else is issued. Collect service crew paperwork if required. Check that you have every page of every document as well as any amendment sheets. Have a look at rally noticeboards for any last-minute amendments, particularly route alterations.

Motoring News B.T.R.D.A.

CAERNARVONSHIRE and ANGLESEY MOTOR CLUB

J.J. BROWN MEMORIAL RALLY

98

A.N.W.C.C. and W.A.M.C.

RALLY CHAMPIONSHIP 1982

An adhesive rally-plate is issued to competitors on most rallies of restricted grade upwards.

Make sure you know who's who in the organising team. Make a note of the room number of the Clerk of the Course for possible bribing (we're only joking). Make a note of room numbers of any desirable female members of the organising team (if you navigate for some Finns they will count this as key information!).

Now return to your hotel and plot the route on your maps. It is advisable to do this by yourself in perfect peace although some drivers help by reading out references. When plotted, check everything and ensure that black spots, out-of-bounds areas and service points have been marked.

Now it will probably be your lot to plot the service crew's route too, Many people (including works teams) write a simple service schedule and hand the list of references and times to the service crew so that they can plot their own itinerary. Part of the fun of amateur servicing is that you almost take part in little rallies of your own – but don't get so carried away by your driving that you become a nuisance, either to the rally or to other motorists.

Always set a sensible average speed schedule for your service crew. Mechanics have been injured because of stupid service schedules – a heavily laden service car is not the best vehicle to drive quickly on twisty roads.

Make sure that your service stops are marked up in your own road book and on your map. The service crew *must* be advised of any out-of-bounds areas (organisers will often specify certain roads as prohibited to service crews to avoid annoyance or congestion).

Allow time for a service meeting with your crew – you must check their maps. They need to know where and when you need tyres and fuel.

Incidentally, when leaving rally and service cars parked overnight make sure that as much as possible is locked away. Sadly, stuff does get pinched – even more ghoulishly, things get stolen from cars which have crashed and been abandoned on stages.

Hopefully you and your service crew will find time to eat before the rally but do not waste valuable plotting time on a four-course meal – order sandwiches and coffee in your room if there is any chance of running out of time.

Make sure your driver is not sampling the local brew too enthusiastically and tell him what time he has to get up. Try to send him to bed at a reasonable time and tell him to restrict any love-making sessions to about four hours! Service crews should also be told what time to book a call for.

Take another trip to Rally Headquarters just to make sure that there are no alterations. On an Italian San Remo Rally some years ago the organisers changed the starting time and more than one experienced competitor appeared at the start when the rally had left!

Finally, book early morning calls and go to bed. But *always* take your own alarm clock. The chaos caused by rallies in the reservations areas can also spread to the early morning call department, as many competitors know to their cost.

2. ANNOUNCEMENTS

(a)   The Pace Petroleum/Autosport National Rally Championship is the only British National Rally Championship for 1982 and the regulations have been approved under Permit Number CH/2033.

(b)   The Championship is promoted and organised by Pace Petroleum Limited, Autosport Magazine and RAC MSA Ltd.

(c)   Autosport will be the only official Newsletter of the Championship. Competitors should refer to this publication for all official information on the Championship. Regular points positions will be printed in Autosport. Queries regarding allocation of points should be referred to Martin Liddle, Tynemouth Computer Services, 27 Garforth Close, Southfield Green, Cramlington, Northumberland. Telephone (0670) 712624 (H).

(d)   Organisers of qualifying events retain the sole right to select and accept entries for their event and the Championship organisers cannot be held responsible for the refusal of an entry.

(e)   In the case of any dispute relating to the Championship it will be referred to an adjudicating panel.

3. ELIGIBILITY

Eligibility for the Championship is reserved for the holders of British and Eire Passports who are also subjects of these countries and who hold suitable Competition Licences issued by the RAC Motor Sports Association Ltd. or RIAC. Competitors who do not fulfil these requirements but who can satisfy either a UK or Eire residential period of five years may apply for consideration of entry. The organisers reserve the right to refuse an entry.

4. REGISTRATION

(a)   All drivers are required to register in order to score points.

(b)   All co-drivers are required to register, but score points *only* when accompanying a registered driver.

(c)   A registration fee of £5.00 is payable to PACE PETROLEUM LTD.

(d)   In applying for registration, a competitor agrees to be bound by these rules and agrees to display two Championship Decals on the car on *all* qualifying events. These decals are supplied by the promoters on registration and will be freely available at all Championship events or on request from the Championship Co-Ordinator. It

19.   The number of persons in the car shall not be varied during the event except when the car is stationary or by official instruction or in the case of an injured person being transported.

20.   If the entrant is not an occupant of the car, the first named driver on the entry form shall be deemed to be his agent.

21.   The Promoters of the Meeting may permit a change of either one driver or the car, but not both, on written application being made by the entrant before scrutineering.

D. ELIGIBLE CARS

22.   An entrant is deemed to have full knowledge of his/her car and to vouch for its eligibility by the act of presenting the car for scrutiny at the start.

23.   The entry will be divided into classes as follows:
Group 1: Standard Touring Cars. (F.I.A. Appendix J Group 1)
Group 2: Modified Touring Cars. (F.I.A. Appendix J Group 2)
Group 3: Standard Grand Touring Cars. (F.I.A. Appendix J Group 3)
Group 4: Modified Grand Touring Cars. (F.I.A. Appendix J Group 4)
Group 5: Specially constructed vehicles and 4 wheel drive vehicles.
Cars of Groups 1 and 3 will be classified under 5 classes, according to their cylinder capacity.
Class 1: Up to 1150 cc.   Class 4: 1601 to 2000 cc.
Class 2: 1151 to 1300 cc.   Class 5: Over 2000 cc.
Class 3: 1301 to 1600 cc.
Cars of Groups 2 and 4 will be classified under 2 classes, according to their cylinder capacity.
Class 1: Up to 1600 cc.
Class 2: Over 1600 cc.
Cars of Group 5 will be classified under one class covering all capacities, as will 4 wheel drive vehicles.

24.   Should there be less than 4 entrant cars in a cylinder capacity, this class will be amalgamated with the immediately higher class. If the incomplete class is the highest one, the corresponding trophy will not be awarded. A group of less than 4 cars will compete only for the general classification.

25.   All cars must be equipped with hand-operated fire extinguishers of at least 5kgs. in no more than two separate units.

26.   It is compulsory to fit a safety roll-over-bar for all specially constructed vehicles and is recommended for all classes.

27.   The addition of sump or chassis guards is permitted.

28.   All cars must be equipped with a first aid kit and mud flaps at the driving wheels.

E. FINAL DOCUMENTATION AND SCRUTINEERING

29.   All crews must report personally, with their car, to scrutineering and documentation at the time and place notified in the additional supplementary regulations.

30.   The following documents must be produced:
a)   Identification cards or passports for both members of the crew.
b)   Valid driving licences.
c)   Valid F.I.A. entrants and drivers licences.
d)   A copy of the registration card for the car.
e)   Evidence that the entrant has third party insurance cover.

31.   Crews must report for scrutineering and documentation at the time specified in the final instructions, under penalty of exclusion.

32.   Rally identification plates and stickers as detailed elsewhere in these regulations will be available prior to each event from a venue notified in the additional supplementary regulations. These must be affixed before presenting the car to scrutineering.

Regulations for Rally Championships are often published in booklet form. Above are pages from (left) a National Rally Championship in the UK, and (right) the Rothmans Middle-East Rally Challenge: the latter regulations are also printed in Arabic.

Caernarfonshire & Anglesey M.C.

J.J. BROWN MEMORIAL RALLY

ADDITIONAL SUPPLEMENTARY REGULATIONS

1. The Caernarfonshire and Anglesey Motor Club will promote a restricted permit rally. The J.J. Brown Memorial Rally, on 4/ 5th December, 1982.

2. The meeting will be governed by the General Competition Rules, Standing Supplementary Regulations of the British Motor Sports Council, incorporating the provisions of the international Sporting Code of the F.I.A., these ASR's and any written instruction the promoting club may issue for the event.

3. R.A.C. Permit No. and D.o.E. No - will be advised in the final Instructions.

4. The event is open to fully elected members of the promoting club and the following:-
   1. Registered entrants in the BTDA/ 1300 Rally Championship.
   2. All fully elected members of motor clubs comprising the A.N.W.C.C.
   3. All fully elected members of motor clubs comprising the W.A.M.C.
   Club Membership cards, competition licences, Registration cards, will be inspected at signing on.

5. The event is a qualifying round of the following championships:-
   a) The A.N.W.C.C. Road Rally Championship.
   b) The Motoring News/ BTRDA Rally Championship.
   c) The W.A.M.C. Road Rally Championship. Division One.
   d) The BTRDA 1300 Challenge.

6. The event will start from Wellfield Car Park, Bangor (115/ 582722 1/ 2) and finish in the Caernarfon area. Total mileage will be approximately 180 miles on metalled and unmetalled roads.

Scrutineering and noise testing will begin at 18.00 hours and any competitor not signed on by 22.00 hours will be excluded. Cars will start at one minute intervals and individual times of starting will be notified in the Final Instructions.

All cars will comply with the R.A.C. Tyre and Vehicle Regulations together with the following rules at scrutineering:-

   1. Cars recording over 78 dba on the noise judges meter will NOT be permitted to start.
   2. Any car with body damage as defined in L 4.13.S(t) will NOT be permitted to start.
   3. Cars shall not have more than two auxiliary lamps fitted. In accordance with QH4.
   4. All cars must be fitted with paper or foam air filters.
   5. Competing cars may not show any sign of radio transmitting device.
   6. Seat belts must be worn on all competitive sections (L4.2.1)

The event will contain competetive sections on the public road timed to an accuracy of less than one minute.

Metric Maps Nos. 115, 123 latest editions will be required. Cars will be identified by rally plates supplied by the organisers and fixed to the front and rear sides of the vehicle. It is the competitors own responsibility to affix numbers to the near-side front door, these may be on sale at the start.

---

11.   CONTROLS AND TIMING
The rally will be divided into Road Sections and Special Stages. All Controls other than Passage Controls (P.C.s) will be Time Controls (T.C.s). Each Road Section will be allotted a Target Time and a competitor can calculate his Due Time of Arrival at any T.C. by adding this Target Time to his actual time of departure from the preceding T.C.
On any Road Section following a Special Stage three or four minutes extra will be allowed over the set average speed to account for any delays at the Special Stage Finish.
All Special Stages will have a Bogey Time set at 60 mph and a Target Time set at approximately 30 mph (or less on short stages).
Competitors will receive penalties as follows :
(i)   Under Bogey .... Bogey Time
(ii)   Over Bogey - under Target .... Actual Time taken
(iii)   Over Target .... Target Time (no extra time penalties)

The following titles shall describe the various types of Controls :
a)   Main Contols (M.C.).
   (i)   Main Controls will be situated at the start and finish of the rally and immediately before and after any Rest Halt.
   (ii)   At the M.C. after the Rest Halt, competitors will restart at one minute intervals in the order in which they 'BOOKED IN' at the Main Control before the Rest Halt. Competitors are reminded, however, that they will be penalised for completing the Road Section before lunch in less than the Target Time.
   (iii) Each competitor will be given a due starting time from any M.C. and the difference between this time and his actual starting time will be counted towards exclusion for overall lateness.
   (iv)   Competitors not excluded by reason of having accumulated more than the maximum allowed lateness will restart (subject to 11(iii) above) from any M.C. with zero lateness, i.e.: lateness is accumulated between two adjacent M.C.s.

b)   Special Stage Arrival Controls (SSA).
   On arrival at SSA a competitor will receive an arrival time only when he is ready to start the stage (helmets on, etc.). He must then proceed immediately to the Start Line. A competitor who is early may wait for his Due Time.

c)   Special Stage Start Control (SSS).
   At the SSS competitors will receive a start time for the Stage in hours and minutes. Once a competitor has clocked in at a SSA, the Start Marshal will assume he is ready to start the Stage and will issue a time as soon as the start line is clear, whether the competitor is ready to start or not. The Marshal will inform the competitor at 15 seconds to go, and at 5 seconds he will hold a flag ahead of the driver. He will count down 5-4-3-2-1 and raise the flag at zero.
   As each section is timed separately, the time taken from SSA to SSS is 'Dead Time' and delays are automatically allowed for. The control area between SSA and SSS will be 'parc ferme'.

Two pages of regulations for typical 'club' rallies. (Left) the 'J.J.Brown Memorial' road rally and (right) the 'Goodyear Lakeland-Ford' stage rally.

MORECAMBE CAR CLUB LTD.
23rd ILLUMINATIONS RALLY
19th/20th FEBRUARY 1983

ENTRY FORM

To be sent, complete in every detail, to:
Nicolette Bye, 17 Dalton Square, Lancaster LA1 1PL.
BLOCK LETTERS PLEASE AND USUAL CHRISTIAN NAMES

Entrant .... Entrant's Lic. No. ....

....

Driver .... Comp. Lic. No. ....

Address .... Tel. No. ....

....

Navigator .... Comp. Lic. No. ....

Address .... Tel. No. ....

Only Entrants holding an RAC Licence will be mentioned in any publicity for the rally.

Make of Car .... Model ....

Reg. No. .... Colour ....

Capacity .... c.c.   Club ....

Class entered : EXPERT / SEMI-EXPERT / NOVICE   *(delete as necessary)*

I am registered in the following Championships:

BTRDA	DRIVER		NAVIGATOR
BTRDA 1300	DRIVER		NAVIGATOR
ANCC	DRIVER		NAVIGATOR

Please tick the boxes as appropriate.

A typical entry form. This is for Morecambe C.C.'s "Illuminations Rally".

CAERNARFONSHIRE AND ANGLESEY MOTOR CLUB
J. J. BROWN MEMORIAL RALLY - 1982
OFFICIAL ENTRY LIST

Championships - A - A.N.W.C.C. Road Rally Championship
B - B.T.R.D.A. Road Rally Championship
b - B.T.R.D.A. 1300 Challenge
W - W.A.M.C. Road Rally Championship

Car No.	ENTRANT AND/OR SPONSOR Driver/Navigator	ABbW	Club	Car reg No.	C.C. Colour
	EXPERTS				
1	GENERAL MOTORS DEALER SPORT Terry Benson/Derek Fryer	B	BTRDA	Vauxhall EXX 888T	2279 White
2	Derek Carless/Peter Forrester	AWB	BTRDA/PAN	Ford RSI800 TUJ I8IS	I794 White
3	E.A.R.S. Mike Pattison/David Taylor	WB/B	BTRDA	Ford RS 1800 RUR 17W	1998 White
4	MICK BRIANT PRODUCTS Mick Briant/Barry Cooper	B	BTRDA/ CRAVEN	Ford RS 1800 KHC 807V	2000 White
5	CITY SPEED (GLOUCESTER) Roger Moran/Tony Beddoes	B	BTRDA	Ford RS 2000	1993 Red
6	RPM Motors (Leominster)/N W C C Peter Gerbez/Gareth Jones	WB/B Herefordshire	N.W.C.C.	Ford RS RCR 867S	1993 White
7	Alistair Sutherland/Nigel Harris			Vauxhall	2000
8	MICK BRIANT RALLYING LTD Steve Hill/Dave Kirkham	WB	BTRDA	Sunbeam AFO 719V	2194 Black
9	HEREFORDSHIRE MOTOR CLUB Kevin King/Phil Jones	W	Herefordshire	Ford RS2000 BNB 660T	1998 White
10	G.M. DEALER TEAM Clive Sisson/Kevin Savage	B	BTRDA	Vauxhall NFR 301X	2300 Red
11	Brian Price/Wyn Morris	W	Brecon/CAMC	Ford	White
12	Tony Hornett/John Youd	AWB	Chester BTRDA	Ford RS OAW 700G	1993 Blue
13	T.B.A John Kiff	WB	Herefordshire		
14	ABP MOTORSPORT John Edwards-Parton/Rod Palmer	B	BTRDA	Sunbeam JLU 717V	2200 Black
15	F.W. LOWE MOTOR BODIES - CREWE Barry Walker/Alan Tomkinson	B	Ecurie Royal Oak	Ford HJH 42W	2000 White
16	NORTH WALES CAR CLUB Wil Morris/Mike Kidd	AW	NWCC/Bala	Ford RS JFF 901P	1993 Red
17	C A MOTOR CLUB/RHYL & DISTRICT M.C. Kim Reddaway/John E. Jones	A	Rhyl & Dis. CAMC	Ford RS	2100
18	Pete Smith/John Millington	B	BTRDA	Colt	1998 White
19	CSMA NORTH LONDON LTD. Mike Biss/Malcolm Barber		CSMA	Avenger TME 310M	1500 White
20	N W C C LTD./GORDON FORD (C BAY) LTD. Gareth Mawby/Gwyn Mawby	A	NWCC	Ford RS PUX 370R	2000 Yellow
21	N WALES R C /HARLECH & DIST M C D.Whitehurst/G.K.Williams		Harlech	AvengerXMX 720M	1498 Yellow

'Runners and riders' for the J.J. Brown Memorial Rally. This list is sent to all competitors before the start. The information given by crews on their entry form will assist the organisers in allocating starting positions.

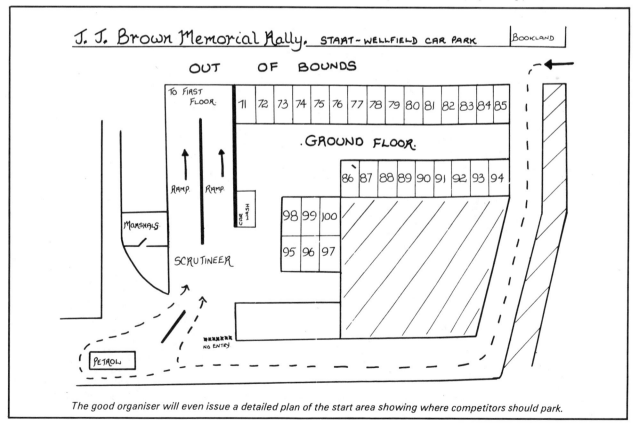

The good organiser will even issue a detailed plan of the start area showing where competitors should park.

EAST BERKS MOTOR CLUB LTD OAKLEAF RALLY

SPECTATOR INFORMATION.

Once again the Oakleaf is here and hopefully it will be as troublefree as in previous years. However we rely on spectators to a great extent not to antagonise the general public as it is difficult for those not involved in the sport to differentiate between spectators and competing cars, so don't upset anybody, drive considerately and keep the noise down at spectator points. Some of thes points are within earshot of peoples homes and bearing in mind that sound carries further at night don't shout to one another along the road.

Listed below there are nine spectator points. If you approach the spectator point as indicated from the nearest A or B road avoiding the roads so specified for rally use you should avoid the rally on minor roads.

We wish you a good nights spectating,

PR Officer, Oakleaf

Grid Ref.	Car 1 Due approx	Spectators App.& Dept
165/E712210S	23.10	West
165,152/SW 648 312 SE	23.35	North East
165,152/NE 740345 NNW	23.50	South West
152/ NW668 356 ENE	00.20	South
First Petrol- Please avoid Farthinghoe.		
152/ S545 419W	01.15	South East, yellow to Brackley.
151/ SE514 487WSW	01.30	North
151/ NE374 392SE	02.11	South West
Second Petrol- Hartwells of Banbury.		
151/ SSE306425WSW	03.50	North
15[illegible]/ [illegible]	04.20	South

Rallies attract spectators and it is important that they do not annoy non-enthusiasts – hence sheets like this.

EAST BERKS MOTOR CLUB OAKLEAF RALLY

STOP JUNCTIONS

A	765 190	
B	690½ 190	
C	673½ 154	
D	653½ 198	(also DIP headlights)
E	663 328½	
F	710½ 317	
G	737½ 332	
H	765½ 335	(also DIP headlights)
I	733½ 361½	
J	6?5 349	
K	613 332	
L	557 357	
M	529 362	
N	518½ 439¾	
O	485 455½	
P	499½ 488¾	
Q	444¾ 474½	
R	412½ 510	
S	384 520	
T	409 417	
U	417½ 377	
V	365¼ 375¾	
W	261 404	
X	285½ 373¾	
Y	355 349	
Z		

The following stop junctions coincide with Time controls. You will be deemed to have stopped at the junction as soon as you have been signed in.

648 226	574¾ 330½	530½ 367½
376¾ 400½	366½ 461¾	430 435
370½ 378½	320¾ 426	263½ 371¾
362 302½	3?0½ 402	

NOTE: DO <u>NOT</u> stop at the following junction.

535½ 419½(Road conditions permitting)

As stated in the final instructions 'Stop Controls' will be in operation at some stop junctions. These should be treated similarly to passage controls; however cars must come to a standstill as near as possible to the white give-way lines on the road and when signed in are free to drive straight off- provided nothing is coming of course! The procedure is the same at Time Controls sited at stop junctions. Other stop junctions will be observed in the usual way.

A key sheet for the co-driver to mark on his map.

Club rally driver Charles Eveson signs on at the start.

CAERNARFONSHIRE and ANGLESEY MOTOR CLUB

J. J. BROWN MEMORIAL RALLY 4/5th DECEMBER 1982

ROUTE CARD

CONTROL	REFERENCE	APP.	DEP.	TARGET	REMARKS
MC 1	582 722½		W		Non competitive to TC 2 - 30 m.p.h. Bangor.
TC 2	648½ 723	NE	WSW	24	
PC 3	620¼ 691¼	NNE	NW		
STC 4	617¼ 678¼	NNE	WSW	12	Non competitive to TC 5. Care along white from VIA to TC 5.
VIA	595½ 711½	SE	SW		
TC 5	594 707	NE	W	7	
PC 6	573½ 681¾	NE	NNW		
PC 7	542¾ 661¼	NW	SSE		
STC 8	513 636	NE	SSW	23	
VIA	504½ 614½	NNE	SW		
VIA	483 601¼	ESE	S		Non competitive to TC 9 - Quiet Bontnewydd, Groeslon, Penygroes and Llanllyfni.
TC 9	462½ 503½	ENE	SW		
PC 10	452 442	NNE	SE		
PC 11	438½ 406¾	SE	NE		
PC 12	458 431	NE	SW		
PC 13	406 411½	NNE	SSW		
STC 14	404½ 372	NE	SW	50	Non competitive to TC 15 IN - VERY QUIET ABERERCH
TC 15 IN	394¾ 380½	SE	NW	4	Time recovery section
TC 15 OUT	393¾ 381½	SE	NW		
PC 16	357¾ 383½	ENE	N		
STC 17	327½ 376¼	NE	SW	12	Non competitive to TC 18. Very quiet RHYDYCLAFDY
VIA	335 360¾	NE	SW		
TC 18	300 347½	ESE	WNW	9	
STC 19	320½ 325½	NNW	S	14	Hand in Time Card Non competitive to Petrol. Fill up with Petrol and proceed to TC 20 IN. Very quiet at Llanbedrog and Abersoch.
PETROL	328½ 317	NW	WNW		

Route instructions for an all night road rally.

SERVICE 'A' TO SS 2 23.47 MILES 48 MINUTES

INTER MILES	TOTAL MILES	LOCALITY	DIAGRAM	INFORMATION
		SV 'A' IN / TARGET 0.10 / SV 'A' OUT	SV 'A' OUT	TARGET 0.48 / SSA 2
0.00	0.00	WEST SHORE		LEAVE SERVICE. RALLY TRAFFIC APPROACHING.
0.05	0.05			
0.08	0.13			PETROL
0.93	1.06	DEGANWY	30	POSSIBLE SPEED CHECK!
1.84	2.90	LLANDUDNO JUNCTION	30	
0.18	3.08	LLANDUDNO JUNCTION		SP CHESTER A55
1.15	4.23			SP BETWS-Y-COED A470
0.70	4.93	GLAN CONWY	30	
9.47	14.40	LLANRWST	30	

On a stage rally, navigation is much simpler. This ia a page from a Gwynedd Rally road book.

MIDAC-ILLUMINATIONS RALLY TIME CARD 1

FAIL TIME	CAR NO.

CONTROL	DIRECTION	SIGNATURE	TIME HOURS	TIME MINS.	TIME SECS.	PENALTY
Start TC1						
SS1						NLP
RC A						
TRC B						
FS 1						
TC 2						
SS 2						NLP
FS 2						
TC 3						NLP
TC 4						
RC C						
TC 5						
TC 6						
TC 7						
TC 8						
RC D						
TC 9						
TC 10						
RC E						
TC 11						
TC 12						
TC 13						
					SUB-TOTAL	

Hand in Time Card 1 at SS 3

A time card ...

Scrutineering Card

CAR NUMBER

		CHECK LIST	✓		Signature
NOISE	QA17	NOISE LEVEL 78 dB MAX.			
BODY WORK	QA2	SHARP EDGES PROTECTED		Noise	
		MUDGUARDS/SPATS		Scrutineer	
TYRES & WHEELS	QA9	TYRE TREAD DEPTH		Scrutineer	
	QA8	SPACERS & STUDS			
LIGHTING QH3		SPOTS CENTRE HEIGHT 24 In.		Club Card	
		SPOTS EDGE SPACING 350mm			
		SIDELIGHTS/FLASHERS		RAC Comp Licence	
		TAIL & STOP LIGHTS			
		NUMBER PLATE LIGHT		Insurance	
		REVERSE LIGHT/WARNING			
		DIPPING - SPOTS WITH HEADS		Signed on	
PASSENGER COMPARTMENT	QA7	STEERING PLAY			
	QA6	BRAKE PEDAL TRAVEL/H'BRAKE		Road Book	
	QH4	RED WARNING TRIANGLE		Time Cards	
	QA3	SEAT SECURE (Non-Tip)		Service	
	QA13	FUEL LINES GUARDED		Road Book	
	QA10	WATER LINES MARKED		DAMAGE AT START	
	QH4(b)	WIPERS WASHERS HORN			
	QA2	PROTECTIVE BULKHEAD			
BONNET & BOOT	QA14	BATTERY LEADS MARKED			
		NO LOOSE FUEL CANS			
	QH2(c)	SPARE WHEEL SECURE			
	QH1	THROTTLE RETURN SPRING			
STAGE EVENTS	QH8	LAMINATED WINDSCREEN			
	QH10	C/HELMETS BS2495 (RAC sealed)		Continued overleaf	
	QH7	FIRE EXTINGUISHER (S) – 5 Kg.			

... and a scrutineering card.

EAST BERKS   M.C.   OAKLEAF RALLY   JAN 7/8

HANDOUT 6   TC 7— TC 10 IN COMPETITIVE

NE   655¾   147½ N
WSW 661   177¾ N
ESE 636½ 200 NNE   TO TC 10 IN

THEN LINK TO TC 10 OUT;   QUIET MARSH GIBBON

EAST BERKS M.C.   OAKLEAF RALLY   JAN 7/8

HANDOUT 10   TC 19 OUT —TC 21 COMPETITIVE

TO TC 21

EAST BERKS M.C. OAKLEAF RALLY   JAN 7/8

HANDOUT 14   TC 28 OUT TO   SECOND PETROL
COMPETITIVE VIA:

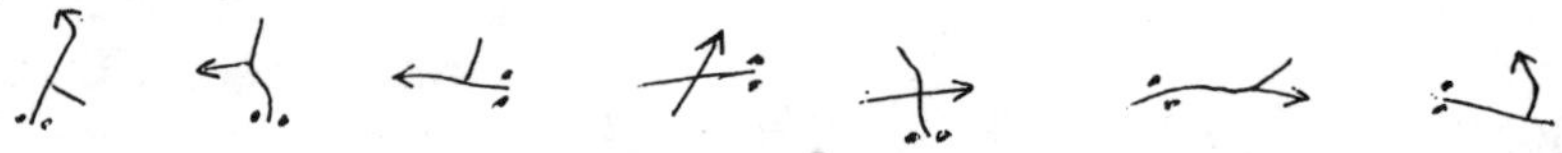

TO   TC 30 IN

THEN COMPETITIVE VIA:

ESE 417¼ 478 NNE
SW 431   495½ NNW
E   384   519¾ SSE
NE 376¾ 490½ SE
N   354   431¼ E

TO TC 37 IN. THEN LINK, QUIET TO TC 37 OUT

THEN COMPETITIVE VIA:

WNW 387½ 385½

141   115   158   157 NNE

TO TC 40 IN.

THEN LINK TO PETROL;   QUIET BANBURY.

On this road rally co-drivers were kept on their toes and had to cope with route instructions handed out in several different ways – these are just three of the sheets given out. Note the detailed directions of approach and departure specified with map references.

No	Driver / Navigator	Club	Cham	STC 4	STC 8	STC 14	PC 17	STC 18/19	lgt 19	STC 21	22–29	STC 30	31	32 33
28	P SPENCER / I WOOLLEY			3.06	7.00	8.07	4.07	3.04	25.24	5.02		11.51		
29	NON-STARTER													
30	J ROBERTS	NON-STARTER												
35	W L PIERCE / M WILLIAMS	NNCC NNCC	A A	3.47	6.50	9.13	3.35	2.57	26.22	5.01		12.33		
36	H EVANS / G M HUGHES	CAMC/NNCC NNCC		3.03	5.27	6.59	3.19	2.10	20.58		R E T I R E D			
37	J H JORDAN / J JONES	CAMC CAMC		4.50	7.48	13.12	4.49	4.04	34.43	7.19		F	F	
38	A L SPENCER / R KENRICK	M.NIRAL NALLISEY	A A	3.51	5.24	6.34	3.11	2.35	21.35	7.38		8.37		
39	M ROYAL / J ORDFORD	CAMC CAMB									R E T I R E D			
40	G EVANS / G BEER	HDMC HDMC		3.38	1.53						R E T I R E D			
41	M BRADD / S GRIFFITHS	PAN PAN	D D	4.07	7.28	10.12	4.11	3.43	29.44	5.20		15.53		
42	E BLACKWELL / I MARSHALL	NNCC CVMC/NNCC		3.16	7.02	6.13	3.39	3.18	23.28	4.50		11.21		
43	W WILLIAMS / M HOLMES	CHESTER		3.30	12.00	7.06	3.11	2.59	25.46	5.50		12.45		
44	J G ROBERTS / I.T THOMAS	BHAINNCC UVMC	AN								N O N - S T A R T E R			
45	P MOULES / A ROE	CSMA NNCC		3.43	11.01	7.26	3.20	6.03	31.35	5.17		12.03		
46	R JONES / R PUGH	TVMC		5.22	F	15.29	4.19	3.50 IF	29.00	7.32		F	F	
47	M ATHERTON / J R JONES	HDMC HDMC									R E T I R E D			
48	P KELSALL / A HANKE	CHESTER CHESTER	AWB ANB	3.18	9.06	6.26	3.07	2.56	24.53	4.44		14.15	F	
49	K HASKINS / K HUGHES	NNCC NNCC		3.48	7.30	10.59	11.21	3.46	37.24 F	F	F F F	F	F F	
50	C EVANS / N WILLIAMS	RHYL RHYL		4.57							R E T I R E D			
51	I WILLIAMS / D ROBERTS	BALAIRHYL BALA	A	4.28	8.34						R E T I R E D			
52	NON-STARTER													
53	Q CORNES / G BELSHAW	ST HEL ST HEL		4.56	7.38	9.53	4.57	3.37	30.44	5.18		F	F	
54	H B WILLIAMS / A MARCHBANK	HDMC CHESTER	A	4.03	7.03	12.51 F	3.46	3.20 IF	31.03	10.19		F		
55	G W WILLIAMS / A JONES	HDMC HDMC	A								R E T I R E D			
56	E FEUTCH / E PRITCHARD	HDMC HDMC		5.06	7.58	10.45	4.08	3.41	31.38	5.30	R E T I R E D			
57	T GROVES / K JONES	RHYL RHYL	A	4.46	7.49	13.04	4.50	5.33	34.02	5.30		F	F F	
58	G McQUILLING / J O'NEILL	NNCC/HDMC HDMC	A								R E T I R E D			
59	N PARRY / H JONES	CAMC CAMC		3.47	5.58	10.30	4.00	3.30	27.45	5.30		18.43		
60	M VAREJ / P CRAVEN	b b		4.53	7.39	9.54	6.38	4.06	33.10	6.40		17.53		
61	NON-STARTER													
62	J APPLETON	CAMC		4.36	8.16	17.37 F	4.42	F	2F 35.11	7.53		20.17		

The rally doesn't end at the finishing line – the results should be studied to see if the organisers' marks agree with yours – but DO NOT become a barrack room lawyer trying to win rallies by post-rally protests. Note 'F' = fail.

Day of rally:

Get up, get dressed (we'll spare you the ablutionary details) and collect together all necessary documents, ignition keys, crash helmets and if supplied (a very important item) the start card. Many organisers issue a start card at scrutineering which must be produced before you can start the rally.

Be at your car in good time, at least fifteen minutes before the start; many rally cars are the very devil to start on a cold, icy morning after a night in an exposed car park.

During the rally you should keep a detailed note of stage times together with other competitors' times. Don't blab too much to the other competitors but keep a running total of all the times and compare them with the organisers' whenever they publish a list. You will often find intermediate results displayed at main controls during the event. If these times and yours do not agree, do not get in too much of a tizzy as there are often mistakes in these results, which are usually telephoned through from Rally Headquarters and presented simply as a guide.

Apart from the usual navigational duties, (covered in detail elsewhere) allow yourself the luxury of a glance at the awards page in the regulations if you think you might be in with a chance, but this should be at a very late stage in the rally, probably on the run in. Many superstitious co-drivers refuse to look at that page until the car is locked up at the finish!

A good co-driver will be totalling his penalties on the run-in to the finish so that he is ready to check the totals when official results are announced. Make sure the car is left where it should be, i.e. in the finish compound; if there is any likelihood of winning a major or class award then it may have to be scrutineered for eligibility (this happens mostly on Internationals).

When you re-enter the hotel/rally headquarters keep the driver away from the bar for a while — radio interviews with winners (well, you *may* have won) don't sound so good with slurred speech.

As soon as the results are announced you should check them with your records. Make sure they tally. If there is a figure with which you disagree you should check with the organisers to see if it is their mistake or yours. Stay within reach of the results room (stages are often cancelled or reinstated and this can alter the results dramatically). If your times do not agree, or if you do not agree with one of the organisers' decisions regarding a cancelled or reinstated stage, don't start shouting and protesting too readily. By all means, check with the organisers and make your point but study your case *very* carefully before considering protesting. *If* you feel very badly done by, then you may feel you *have* to protest but *please don't* become a barrack room lawyer bickering and protesting about trivialities. The place to win rallies is in the car.

If you look like winning, then make sure that you and your driver know where the presentation is to be held. Make sure that your driver goes to it; it is not unknown for winning drivers to be missing when awards are presented. This is the height of bad manners; you owe it to organisers, spectators, fellow competitors and marshals to be there. If you win, you will probably be expected to make a speech. Be succinct and genuine. You will not be expected to be witty or particularly eloquent, but obey some protocol — if there are Mayors, Lordships or whatever else present, then start your speech properly. Always thank the Club, the organisers and marshals, whatever your personal feelings. Never knock other competitors and try to appear as humble as possible without overdoing it.

Your work is now over, and you can let all those regulations, figures and numbers fade into oblivion. You may now find their place taken by more useful numbers — like the phone number of that lady you met at signing on ...

10 How to organise a rally

If you want a really thankless task, organise a rally. You will spend hundreds of hours in hard, tiring and frustrating work, only to have your results greeted with last-minute disappointments, abuse and possibly even protests.

However, we mustn't deter potential rally organisers because the sport literally depends on competent, efficient enthusiasts prepared to undertake the work.

One chapter in a book of this size can hardly offer a complete guide for organisers, but it can highlight most of the important steps to be taken when organising a rally. Remember, as the organiser of an average Restricted rally you will be catering for a hundred or more of the most agile minds in the sport, and they'll be ready to pounce on any small loophole that presents itself. So you must be on your toes from the moment you start to lay plans for a rally.

It would be unwise for a club to give the sole responsibility for organising an event to a complete beginner. Far more sensible to let a person gain experience by allowing him to understudy an established organiser before taking the reins himself.

Probably the first thing to look at from a club's point of view is the *reason* for running a rally. It is no good running a rally as a means of swelling club funds, or as a means of putting a club on the map. Probably the main reason for running a rally will be to help complete the club's calendar and give members a varied and full year of motor sport.

Having decided to run a rally, the club must decide whether to run a stage or road event. Numerous factors will have a bearing on the decision but the most likely will be the availability and type of terrain in which the club finds itself. Another guiding factor will be the relative popularity of the two types of event.

Although it must be the aim of every organiser to run a perfect rally with no mistakes, perfect events are few and far between. Even some of the world's major rallies make mistakes in regulations or paperwork. After all there are a thousand-and-one things for an organiser of a rally to remember; nevertheless, every organiser should strive for perfection.

A club will need a small team or committee of people to organise an event, the size of the team depending on the size and nature of the rally. Generally speaking, stage rallies require greater manpower and are probably more difficult for the beginner to organise although the organiser of a road rally may meet his share of problems during the route authorisation stage, unless he is very lucky.

However, assuming that you are going to organise a road rally, fix the date and duration of the event. Selecting the date can be difficult; it is no good running a rally if it is going to clash with another event on the same night. If the route clashes in the same area then you will not be able to run your rally, and if the event clashes with one in a different area, then you will probably not attract entries. So great care must be taken in selecting a suitable date.

It will be necessary to apply for a date through your local Regional Association's "dates meeting". Most of the better established rallies have a traditional date, so if you plan to use the same area keep away from their dates. You must keep six weeks away from any club running in your patch.

Naturally an organiser must have a good idea of the time of year he plans to run the rally. Some of the factors that might influence a date choice are the hours of darkness at a given time of year, the condition of unsurfaced tracks during different seasons or any regional peculiarities, like the presence of holiday-makers.

At a very early stage you will have to decide on the area in which you plan to run the rally, bearing in mind most of the best rally territory is already well spoken for. It is best to run a rally in your own area

RAC MOTOR SPORTS ASSOCIATION LIMITED
APPLICATION FOR A PERMIT

Name of Organising Club(s)...

Date of Event .... Date of Practice (if different) ....

Status of Event .... Venue ....

The above club(s) applies for a Permit to organise the following event, which will be held under the General Regulations of the RAC Motor Sports Association Ltd (incorporating the provisions of the International Sporting Code of the FISA), any subsequent requirements of the RAC MSA and the Supplementary Regulations overleaf.

TYPE OF EVENT:
(please tick appropriate boxes)

CAR RACE R	SPEED S	OFF-ROAD X	KART RACE K
	Sprint	Autocross	Kart Circuit
	Hill Climb	Rallycross	Long Circuit
	Drag Race	Grass Track	
		2CV/Minicross	
RALLY Y	**TRIAL T**	**AUTOTEST A**	**CROSS COUNTRY C**
Road	Sporting		Trial
Navigation	Production		Safari
Economy	Classic		Hill Rally
Stage			Timed Trial
Single Venue			Orienteering
Road 12 Car			

In the following form, please complete all sections indicated by the code letter for the type of event being organised plus all sections which have no code letter.

Secretary of the Meeting

Name.. Signature ....

Address... Date ....

....

Phone (Day) .... (Evening)..

Valid from 1.1.81.

SUPPLEMENTARY REGULATIONS

1. The Supplementary Regulations issued to competitors must be exactly in accordance with those shown below, with no change in either wording or order.

2. All blank spaces in the sections appropriate to the type of event should be completed using block capitals or typewriter.

3. Any words shown in bold type, e.g. **being sponsored by,** should be deleted if inapplicable.

4. Any words shown in brackets, e.g. (L2.5) are for information and should NOT appear in the printed S.R.'s.

5. A separate sheet may be submitted if there is insufficient room to answer any specific question.

6. Where a regulation is only applicable to a specific type of event(s) this is indicated by underlining e.g. Rallies.

7. The Entry Form must comply with Sections D11.2 & D11.3 in the Motor Sports Year Book.

TITLE OF EVENT..

SUPPLEMENTARY REGULATIONS

1. The..Club(s)
will organise a...............................(status) permit...........................(type of event)
on.....................................at....................................(venue or start venue)

2. The meeting will be governed by the General Regulations of the RAC Motor Sports Association Ltd., (incorporating the provisions of the International Sporting Code of the FISA), these Supplementary Regulations and any written instructions that the organising club may issue for the event.

3. RAC MSA Permit Number...........................(this will be supplied with the Permit Advice Note) has been issued.
D.O.E. Authorisation Number ....(or D.O.E. Authorisation has been applied for). Rallies, only.

4. The event is open to:
(a) All fully elected members of the organising club(s).
(b) Members of the following clubs, (or championships, or associations) (D3.1.3)

(c) All competitors holding a valid RAC MSA National or International Competition Licence. (Autotest and Trial – valid RAC MSA licence)
(d) All competitors holding: a valid International Competition Licence.
(note 4(a) applies for Closed and Closed-Joint events, 4(a) and 4(b) for Restricted, 4(c) for National and 4(d) for International events.

5. All competitors and drivers must produce a valid **Competition Licence, Medical Certificate, Club Membership Card, Championship Registration Card** (delete as appropriate).

6. The event is a round of the...championship(s)

7. The programme of the meeting will be:–
Scrutineering starts at..**Individual times for scrutineering will be notified in Final Instructions.**
Any competitor not signed on by..may be excluded
Practising starts at ....
First car starts/First race will be at ....

8. **R K** Car and Kart Race Meetings. There will be..races as follows:
(state length of each race, classes or formulae, whether heats and final, handicap races etc).

(a) All vehicles must comply with RAC MSA Technical Regulations or Kart Technical Regulations (for events up to National Status).
(b) **Competitors in races number**...........................**must produce Homologation forms at Scrutineering and have them available throughout the meeting.**

Organising a rally is a demanding business. Here are just two pages of the application form for a rally permit.

Without marshals there wouldn't be any rallying. Here a stalwart signs on for a hard night's work in Hertfordshire. Note the pre-set clocks, and envelopes packed with marshal's instructions. Control signs will also be issued.

if possible as this makes the marshalling and route work much easier and, in any case, clubs in other areas won't thank you if you invade their area and upset the natives, the police or anyone else.

Among all the other decisions to be made at an early stage will be that of the status of the event. Obviously, novice organisers should start off on twelve car or "closed-to-club" rallies while an experienced team should be able to cope with a closed-joint or Restricted event. Generally speaking, the bigger the event, the better the standard of entry and therefore the more demanding and critical their requirements.

No rally can be run legally unless the event is 'approved'. The only events that do not have to conform to the Motor Vehicles (Competition and Trials) Regulations, 1969, are 1) events with not more than twelve vehicles, 2) events where there is no route and where competitors are not timed or required to visit places other than a finish venue, 3) road safety events and 4) military training exercises (we know some rally cars are built like tanks – some even handle like them – but they still don't fall in this category).

However, the R.A.C. Motor Sports Association will need details of even a twelve car event before waiving the need for a permit and such events must be classified as either road, navigational, economy or vintage (veteran) on the application form to them. Note that *road* twelve car rallies need a full permit, not a waiver, unlike the other categories. No twelve car rally must be scheduled to run between 18.00 hours on a Saturday and 07.00 on a Sunday and, quite rightly, a prescribed amount of P.R. work is necessary. Details of the route must be supplied to the Rally Liaison Officers (see below).

Assuming that your event requires authorisation then it will be necessary for you to study the statutory regulations and complete the appropriate application forms. These are available from the R.A.C. Motor Sports Association Ltd., 31 Belgrave Square, London SW1X 8QH (01-235-8601) and from the Royal Scottish Automobile Club, 11 Blytheswood Square, Glasgow (041-221-3850).

Before submitting the application and route for authorisation you must make contact with numerous organisations. The Regional Associations of car clubs play a useful role in co-ordinating lists of road information and can often save many wasted hours by giving advice on certain areas to avoid; putting your route through some of these areas can mean almost certain refusal from the rally authorisation department.

Each Regional Association has a Rally Liaison Officer and he has full information available to prevent rally problems. These people have various Police areas and National Parks areas assigned to them and they will make all the necessary contacts initially. They will also advise you.

Organisers of events planning to use British forests should contact the R.A.C.M.S.A's Forestry Liaison Officer for the area. These unpaid enthusiasts have great knowledge of the working of the forests within their area and clubs *must* channel all their enquiries through them – not to the Forestry Commission direct.

From the above you will probably gather that the R.A.C.M.S.A. is doing everything in its power to keep the peace between rallyists and the authorities. They are generally successful but there are some areas in Britain (and the rest of the world) where rallies are far from welcome.

Anyway, after the informal approaches have been cleared, you are ready to submit your application for authorisation. Read Schedule 3 of the Statutory Regulations to make sure that your event complies fully with them. There are seventeen separate standard conditions which the event must fulfil, most of which concern the routing and timing of the event. If the event does not comply with the standard conditions then the organiser and competitors can face a fine of £50 under Section 36 of the Road Traffic Act 1962.

When the application form is sent in to the authority, two copies of a tracing from the appropriate 1:50,000 scale Ordnance Survey Map (quarter inch O.S. map in the case of Scotland) must also be submitted. The tracings must contain full details of the route together with details of timing and controls.

It may seem unnecessary to submit an application six months before an event but it can take a long time to gain authorisation, particularly if there are any route clashes when the R.A.C. will suggest re-routes and tracings will fly back and forth between authorisers and organisers.

It will be necessary to pay an *authorisation* fee should your event be given the green light. This is based on the number of vehicles taking part and upon the length of event. It can range from £1.20 to £5.80 per vehicle. An R.A.C. recognised club will also require an R.A.C. permit. Once a club is recognised by the R.A.C. it agrees to be bound by rules and regulations that are laid down in the R.A.C. Motorsport Regulations and updated each year in their Year Book. The Year Book deals with all forms of motor sport and has a section purely devoted to rallies where requirements and standard conditions are laid down. The R.A.C. permit provides Third Party legal liability insurance and should be applied for some six weeks or so before the event. The fees for this are again based on a *per capita* basis.

Talking about insurance, remember that most private insurance policies no longer give cover for rallies and so the R.A.C's brokers have devised a scheme whereby individuals can obtain road traffic cover for the duration of an event. The administration of this insurance must be done through the organising club and the brokers issue a block cover note for the event. The R.A.C. will give details of this insurance, together with another policy which insures officials during an event (providing they have all signed a special form).

In the previous paragraphs we have implied that the event to be organised is a road rally; certainly these can be more complicated in the authorisation application stages. Similar procedures will have to be followed by the organisers of a stage rally although there will, of course, need to be more liaison with individual land-owners. Permission from land-owners will have to be submitted to the authorisation department and it will be necessary to obtain land-owners' indemnity insurance, as well as the other insurances.

Whatever the size of an event, a club will need to form a committee of keen enthusiasts, all of whom should be perfectionists with a real love for the sport.

The committee should have a chairman who should establish general principles and make the major decisions; ideally he should be experienced in rallying, either as organiser or competitor. However, perhaps the most important post is that of the Clerk of the Course who will be responsible for the route-finding, together with the time schedules and general layout of the event. The Secretary of the Meeting will be responsible for most of the paperwork – production of regulations and so on – as well as for administration during the event and maybe the results team too. An Entry Secretary is a useful addition to the team as he can take one onerous chore away from the Secretary.

A number of co-ordinators, or Sector marshals should be appointed; they will look after certain sections of the route and be able to make emergency decisions in their area on the day of the rally.

In the case of a stage rally a Commander should be appointed for each stage to take control of that section – his counterpart in road rallies will be in charge of a group of controls; great experience is necessary for these people as they can make or mar an event.

A Public Relations Officer is most important as he is the person who makes written and personal contact with many of the people who may well be opposed to the rally. He will need a lot of assistance and ideally should lead a team of articulate, knowledgeable people who will attempt to iron out any route-finding P.R. problems at an early stage, by calling on land-owners and householders before (and in some cases after) the event.

Much of the work takes place *before* the event but on the day or night of the rally it will be

Scrutineering will often be more for safety than homologation purposes. Here a scrutineer checks helmets ...

absolutely essential to have another important person, the Results Marshal. He should head a team organised to produce speedy, accurate results – these will probably be fed in from various sections of the route by telephone and confirmed by completed documents as the rally progresses.

Naturally, computers can be used in the calculation of results and of course are frequently used for the major rallies, but beware. Unless you have a professional programmer and operator involved steer well clear of computers, for a few wrongly applied penalties can soon have the opposite effect to speeding up the results!

Other posts which are important though the level may vary according to the size of the event, are Medical Officer, Chief Safety Officer, Programme Officer, Chief Timekeeper, and Equipment Officer. All events will also require a Scrutineer and Stewards and these people *must* be fully qualified and fully acquainted with their duties; don't just appoint people under the Old Pals Act. Note that there should be enough scrutineers to avoid queues building up.

Organisers of special stage rallies will need to

pay particular attention to medical aspects and in addition to the Chief Medical Officer other medically qualified people should be available and positioned properly. Accidents happen and a stage rally organiser must cover every detail so that any accidents can be dealt with efficiently. Doctors, ambulances, fire appliances and breakdown teams must be available to get to any section quickly and everybody must be aware of the various channels of communication.

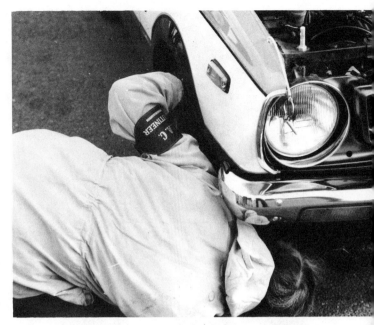

... Wheel bearings ...

... Tyre condition ...

Having planned everything in the utmost detail before the event the rally organiser must then be prepared for numerous last-minute changes. Many rally organisers have suddenly found sections of their route impassable because of floods, ice, snow or fallen trees, and competent people must be available to make re-routes and support them with written documentation literally minutes before the arrival of the first car.

Incidentally it makes sense to have someone delegated to promote the event and get publicity for it – if sponsors are involved they may be able to help here. They must liaise with local newspapers and radio stations by supplying them with details of interesting entries etc. They will not only be carrying out a valuable P.R. service for your club and your event, but also for rallying as a whole. They must liaise with any local civic dignitary or Beauty Queen who may be called upon to start the event. In addition they may get involved with the printing of the programmes and a number of very important details which contribute towards the success of an event.

Try not to combine the media promotion with the task of doing P.R. with farmers and householders along the route: they are different

... and seat mountings. Lights will, of course, be checked before a night rally.

jobs. Both are important and need individual attention.

Now let us consider the rally documents. All road books, route cards, time cards and other printed matter must be of high quality, easily read and understood. Be particularly clear and concise in wording instructions and let there be no excuse for misunderstandings. We appreciate that not all rally budgets will run to beautifully printed documents but ordinary duplicating or Xerox prints will be quite satisfactory; just make sure that every sheet handed out is totally readable.

Whatever the weather, spectators will gather. And all ages too!

The chapter on rally navigation covered the different types of route instruction; a straightforward list of map references, with directions of approach and/or departure is the most popular form for a road rally. Incidentally, check everything that is printed — a small printer's error could produce absolute chaos with your entire rally entry bogged down in a field!

For special stage rallies the route should be given out in the form of a Tulip road book. Some organisers think that this is not totally necessary and that a few map references will suffice but when competitors are required to visit some stages more than once confusion can easily be caused by the navigator having too many lines on his map. Tulip arrows are simple to prepare and simple to read. Organisers will probably need to make at least two complete trips round the route to collect all the junction diagrams, distances and signpost directions. All junctions and mileages should be put into order and clearly typed, preferably with a clear faced typewriter. The road book must give the competitor all the information for him to complete the route. Like everything else in rallying, the clearer and simpler the better.

In addition to the route, the road book should contain details of relevant telephone numbers, list of controls and special stages, service and rest halts and any other useful information. Procedure at special stages should be reiterated and there should also be special notes about damage, and indeed a damage declaration form, as this will enable any route damage to be traced by the organisers, providing a form has been returned to them.

The marking of special stages is a topic that causes great discussion wherever rally crews meet but again, the most sensible guideline is to make sure that everything is marked clearly and without any ambiguity. The R.A.C. demand that a 'Tulip' route or diagram of every stage should be given to competitors and that all junctions are clearly arrowed, unused roads being blocked off by logs or tape.

Advance arrows should be placed approximately 50 yards before a junction (or fire break), but if competitors are likely to be travelling at really high speeds the distance should be increased to give adequate braking distance before the corner.

Arrows on junctions should be placed either side of the road to form a 'gate' through which competitors will pass (be sure to leave them far enough apart so that they do not get knocked over). The arrows should always show the general direction of the exit road using one of the following positions: straight on, 45° right or left, 90° right or

Noise complaints can affect the future of road rallying so all cars have to pass a rigid noise check before and during each event. Here a marshal uses an approved decibel meter.

When a stage has been arrowed and fully set up, at least two cars should travel over the route. One should be driven at a fairly slow speed in order to double check that all is correct and the other should be driven at rally speed to give a competitor's view of things.

Clear reliable time pieces should be used by all marshals and these marshals must be quite clear about their role in the event. They must be familiar with all the time cards which they will have to sign and they must use a consistent method of handling cars. It is no good stage marshals counting some cars down from ten to one, then merely shouting the last three seconds to another car. There must always be an adequate number of marshals at each control and there must be a visual signal at 'go'.

Marshalling is an important part of rallying and we have already advocated that everyone should have a crack at the job, at least once in their life. Marshals control the progress of an event and, be it a road or stage rally, their efficiency can have a tremendous bearing on the success of a rally. Organisers should give as much information as possible to marshals. Such information should tell them about the event, their responsibilities and details of competitors. It must clearly mark responsibilites — a Stage Finish marshal and a Car Park marshal are totally different beings.

Marshalling can be great fun but just occasionally marshals gain something of a power complex and though marshals are generally the much loved, unsung heroes of rallying there are one or two who do little to endear their club to competitors.

We advocated in an earlier chapter that competitors should be nice to marshals; we suggest that this ought to be reciprocated.

Marshals must be absolutely reliable and turn up at briefings and of course control points well in advance of their due times. They should be properly dressed for the occasion and should take plenty of spare clothing as well as umbrellas, spare torches, paper, maps, food and refreshments and anything else that makes the job more comfortable. Marshalling is an interesting job and can be very satisfying as well.

While on the subject of marshals we should at this point mention the paperwork which will have to be issued to them. The Chief Marshal will have the responsibility of having these printed and mailed but will, of course, work under the close eye of the Clerk of the Course for many is the marshal who has found himself experiencing a particularly quiet night as a result of being sent the wrong map reference for a control!

Ideally, each marshal should be posted a detailed diagram of his control and the direction of approach and departure of the rally cars. Some organisers plot the route onto an O.S. map then cut

left and 135° right or left. It is important that the advance arrows and the arrows on the junctions are identical in the direction in which they point. As mentioned, any road that is not being used must be physically blocked off and a "no entry" sign placed several metres into the road in case somebody goes along it by mistake.

When signposting airfields take particular care to make the route as clear as possible as the number of stories of people lost on airfield stages over the years would fill a book twice this size. One little arrow leaning against a straw bale in the centre of a mile-long runway will not be easily picked up on a wet and windy night!

Caution boards are important and should be used by responsible rally organisers though not over-used. Some organisers take the view that "all's fair in love and war" and seem to derive satisfaction from seeing expensive cars drop over rocky ledges. Better organisers will place a caution board where there is an obvious chance that accidents will occur and only the most foolish drivers will ignore such boards.

While on the subject of boards let us mention that flying finish and finish-line boards should be positioned intelligently so that cars have enough room to slow down and stop between a flying finish and the stop line. For International events these boards must be in pairs, positioned on each side of the track.

Morecambe Car Club Ltd

A member of the Association of Northern Car Clubs
and the Association of North East & Cumbria Car Clubs

Please reply to:

S. Lawrenson,
Bell Cottage,
Burton-in-Kendal,
Carnforth.
TEL. (   ) 78167

MORECAMBE CAR CLUB LTD.

ILLUMINATIONS RALLY 19/20 FEBRUARY

This Rally is promoted by the above Club under the rules and guidance of the
Royal Automobile Club. The route of approximately 200 miles has been approved by
the R.A.C. and consequently, permission to run the Rally on this date has been
granted by the Depratment of the Environment. The local Police Authorities,
National Park Board and National Farmers Union also have been informed of the
passage of this event.

We have attempted in the planning of the route to avoid most villages and built-up
areas. All Checkpoints are being manned by efficient marshals and sited away from
dwellings to minimise potential problems. All gates across the roads that are to be
used will be opened and closed by officials, to ensure the safety to stock on the
land.

A representative of the organising Club will be visiting all isolated farmhouses or
dwellings that are close to the route to ensure that residents are aware of the
plans and to assure them that every effort will be made to protect their peace of
mind. Finally competitors will all be notified that any undue nuisance or noise
created by them during the event will mean their instant disqualification from
the event. We know that many people along the route will be taking an interest in
our passage and a great number will be watching the cars go by at several points.

The first competing car should be passing near to your property from .... to
.... at .... and the last one at .... There may be a few minutes
difference in these times either way, but they should not be far off.

May we thank you for your kind indulgence, and suggest that if you have any point
or matter that you would like to raise, you contact us, and we will endevour to
clarify it for you.

We are very fond of our sport, and do not want damage caused to its name for lack
of a little care in preparation.

You may be interested in watching this event yourself, if so please let me know
and I will arrange for you to receive a free copy of the entry list.

SIGNED....N. S. Lawrenson..
          (Chief PR Officer)

Registered Office: 35 Cyprus Road, Heysham, Lancashire, LA3 2QS   Company Registration no: 1398288

Public Relations work is absolutely essential if a road rally is to cause no problems. This is the sort of letter which must be delivered to EVERY householder on the route.

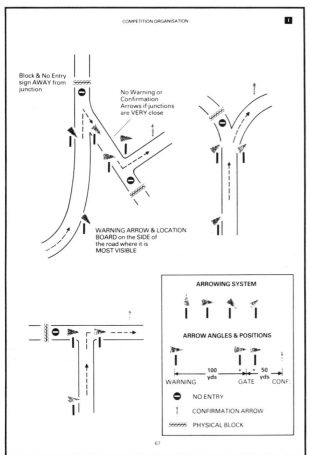

The standard system of arrowing stages is also shown in the Blue Book. *(Reproduced by permission of the RAC MSA)*

COMPETITION REGULATIONS

*4.13.5. Performance will be assessed in one of the two methods listed. The 'Marks Lost' penalties as shown below will apply, *unless they are modified in the SRs, or the SRs specify the 'Fails system'.*

		Marks Lost	or Fails
(a)	Not reporting at a control	300	1
(b)	Not reporting at or providing proof of visiting a check	300	1
(c)	Not complying with a requirement of the Road Book or Route Card	150	1
(d)	Not complying with a reasonable instruction by an Official provided warning is given that a penalty will be applied	150	1
(e)	Not attempting or being ready to attempt a stage or test when instructed to do so	10	plus the highest penalty incurred by any competitor in the class competing the test correctly.
(f)	Not completing a stage or test	10	
(g)	Not performing a stage or test correctly other than as (j)	10	
(h)	Making a false start in a stage or test	60	
(i)	Stopping in a section specified as non-stop	150	
(j)	Striking a barrier, wall, marker or pylon, or crossing the boundary of a test or failing to cross or stop at any line as required in a test (per mistake)	10	
(k)	Every second (and fraction) taken to complete a test or stage (subject to I 2.10.4 and 2.13.10)	1	(and fraction)
(l)	Arriving at or departing from a control or check, other than that at the end of a non-competitive section, before Due time per minute	20	
*(m)	Arriving at a control or check after corrected time – per minute, where timing is to whole minutes – per fraction of a minute, where timing is to a fraction of a minute	10	maximum penalty not to exceed that for (a) missing a control.
**(n)	Early arrival at the end of a non-competitive section	300	1
**(o)	Breach of a Statutory requirement concerning the driving of a motor vehicle or breach of 4.11.1	300	1
**(p)	Contravening 4.10.26	300	1
**(q)	Breach of Technical Regulations concerning the use of lights and breaches of the Construction and Use or Lighting of Vehicles Regulations	300	1
†(r)	Excessive noise	300	1
†(s)	Damaged or ineffective silencing system	300	1
(t)	Damage to car (4.13.6)	100	
††(u)	Receiving assistance contrary to 4.1.4 or 4.7		Road rallies 1800 Marks. Stage Rallies 30 minutes.
(v)	Breach of Regulations 4.6.4, 4.6.6, 4.6.7, 4.6.9, 4.11.3, 4.13.2		Exclusion by Stewards of the Meeting.
†††(w)	Breach of Regulation 4.6.8		Stage max. plus 30 mins.

*Except in 'non-competitive' sections where only a maximum lateness penalty equal to (a) shall be applied. Note requirements for Navigational, Economy and Vintage Rallies.
**These penalties may not be decreased by the Supplementary Regulations, and in each case the Stewards of the Meeting will exclude a competitor committing the offence a second time. Note requirements for Navigational, Economy and Vintage Rallies.
†Causing a decibel reading taken in accordance with the test procedure detailed in the Technical Regulations and the levels laid down in 4.9.2 or such lesser figure as may be specified in the Supplementary Regulations will be deemed excessive noise.
At the discretion of a Judge of Fact any car causing excessive noise may be refused permission to proceed at any time. The penalty for a second offence will be automatic exclusion.
††Second offence exclusion.
†††Any road section penalties thus incurred will be applied up to and including exclusion.

95

The RAC Blue Book *sets out the standard penalty system for rallies. (Reproduced by permission of the RAC MSA)*

---

it up into approximately 4km squares, each featuring a control. These are then pasted onto the marshals' instructions.

The instructions for each control will detail the time due of the first car (in B.B.C. time, to avoid any confusion) and the time of opening the control (usually 30 minutes before the first car is due). The time of closing for the stage is also notified (generally 30 minutes after the time of arrival of the last expected car).

A marshal's check sheet should be sent out with the instructions – this may be incorporated in the instructions, to save printing costs. This sheet will feature a number of ruled lines – one for each car in the rally. The marshals will be required to mark in the time each car visits the control; this document can prove vital if proof of passage of a rally car is required at the finish. Naturally, the sheets should be handed in at the results headquarters.

The starting point of a rally is important if things are to go well. The most used rally start areas are garages or large petrol stations, although more important events may start from City Squares, Promenades or even from the Town Hall steps. Whatever starting facilities are chosen make sure that everything is clear and straightforward for competitors and spectators alike. Obviously it is important to have petrol available near to the start and it is usually not difficult to find a garage which will open specially to offer starting facilities in exchange for the petrol sales. There must be enough room for signing-on and adequate toilet facilities should be available.

How much you dress up the start of your rally depends upon the nature of the event and possibly what sponsorship you have but an informed commentator and P.A. system is always a good thing. Even a few bits of well positioned bunting and a banner or two can add a sense of occasion!

Half-way stops and petrol halts are most important. The rally should be timed to give competitors adequate time for re-fuelling. When selecting a garage for a petrol halt, make sure that they know what they are in for and that they have adequate staff as well as adequate change and all

نهاية مرحلة خاصّة – ٤ مراقبين

FINISH OF SPECIAL STAGE – 4 MARSHALS

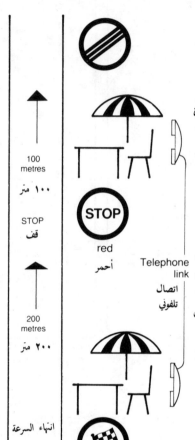

MARSHAL 1 – positioned at flying finish.
Operates clock, i.e. stops it as a car passes the flying finish line (red board) and informs Marshal 2 of the time.

MARSHAL 2 – positioned at flying finish.
Enters car number and the time, as informed by Marshal 1, on the check sheet. Telephone the stop line and informs them of the car number and time. Also answers telephone from stop line regarding any queries of times and consults his check sheet.

MARSHAL 3 – positioned at stop.
Collects timecards from competitor and gives them to Marshal at table. When completed returns them to car.

MARSHAL 4 – positioned at stop.
Enters time, as informed by flying finish line, in competitors time card and stamps the card. Enters any incidents on report sheets.

100 metres
١٠٠ متر

STOP
قف

200 metres
٢٠٠ متر

انتهاء السرعة
Flying finish

100 metres
١٠٠ متر

STOP
red
أحمر

Telephone link
اتصال تلفوني

red
أحمر

yellow
أصفر

المراقب الأوّل – موقفه عند الانتهاء السريع.
يشغّل الساعة، أي يوقفها لحظة مرور سيّارة بخط الإنهاء السريع (للوحة الحمراء) ويخبر المراقب الثاني بالوقت.

المراقب الثاني – موقفه عند الانتهاء السريع.
يقيّد رقم السيارة والوقت على ورقة التقرير عندما يخبره المراقب الأول بالوقت. يتّصل هاتفياً بمراقبي خط الوقوف ويخبرهم برقم السيارة والوقت. يردّ أيضاً على المكالمات الهاتفيّة التي ترد من خط الوقوف فيما يتعلّق بأية استفسارات عن الأوقات ويرجع إلى ورقة التدقيق الخاصة به.

المراقب الثالث – موقفه عند نقطة الوقوف.
يجمع بطاقات الوقت من السائقين ويعطيها للمراقب عند المنضدة. وعند ملئها يعيدها إلى السيّارة.

المراقب الرابع – موضعه عند نقطة وقوف.
يسجل الوقت حسبما يتلقّاه من خط الإنهاء السريع في بطاقة الوقت الخاصة بالمشترك ويختم البطاقة. يدوّن أيّة حوادث على أوراق التقرير.

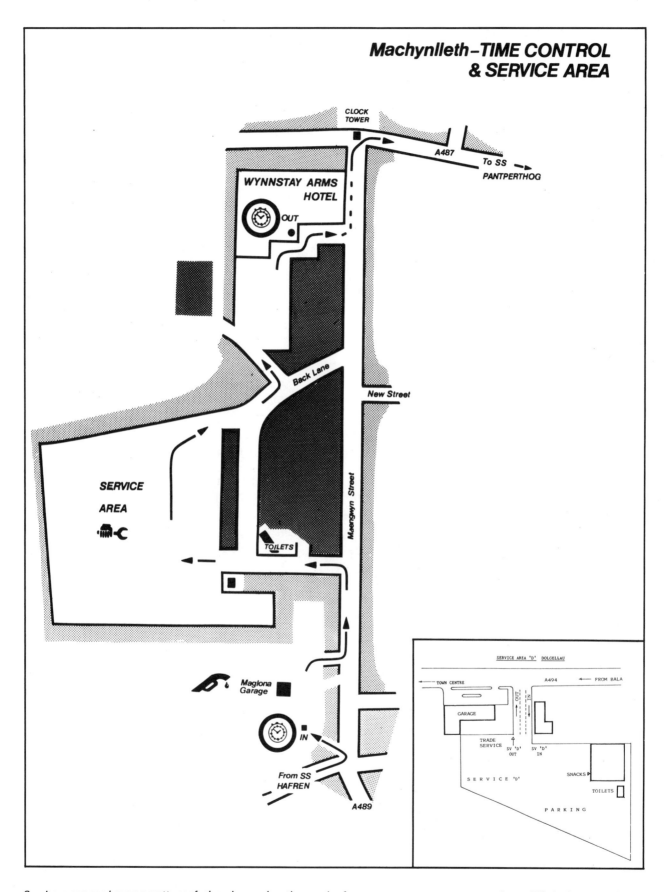

Machynlleth–TIME CONTROL & SERVICE AREA

CLOCK TOWER

A487

To SS PANTPERTHOG

WYNNSTAY ARMS HOTEL

OUT

Back Lane

New Street

SERVICE AREA

Maengwyn Street

TOILETS

Maglona Garage

IN

From SS HAFREN

A489

SERVICE AREA 'D' DOLGELLAU

TOWN CENTRE

A494 ← FROM BALA

GARAGE

OUT

IN

TRADE SERVICE

SV 'D' OUT

SV 'D' IN

SERVICE 'D'

SNACKS

TOILETS

PARKING

Service areas can become pretty confusing places when thousands of spectators turn up so most organisers will help the competitor find his way round. These examples are from the Lombard-RAC and Gwynedd Rally roadbooks.

necessary facilities. Remember, too, that service cars and spectators will probably wish to fill up, so the petrol pump attendant should not be surprised if his two-pump/wooden shack emporium takes on the appearance of a motorway service station for a while.

Organisers should send someone to petrol halts *well* in advance of the rally — one important event collapsed at 3a.m. when the garage owner forgot to open up!

In the case of an all-night rally the hotel or restaurant selected for the finish must have adequate catering and washing facilities and good car-parking space. Motorway service areas are often used although these can be a little impersonal and the rally prizegiving can lose something of its glamour if held in the corridor between the Transport Cafe and the "Gents".

In the case of bigger rallies where competitors and officials will be staying the night, it is important to have a good working relationship with hotels selected as starting or finishing points. Many hotel groups now actively encourage rallies to start and finish at their premises.

When the rally has disappeared, all signs of it should have similarly vanished. The sport of rallying will not endear itself to the general public if it leaves a string of empty oil-cans and old racing numbers in its wake.

A good rally can be ruined if results take a long time to appear so it is important that a smooth system is developed to produce results and to keep competitors furnished with information about their performance as the event progresses. Most rallies use telephone links between their headquarters and personnel in the field. It is sensible to put up lists of penalties at frequent intervals at the rally finish to keep people interested until the full results are posted. Printed sets of results should be mailed to all competitors as soon as possible after the event and it is a courtesy to send them to all the marshals and other interested parties.

Rally organisers are a masochistic breed but, on the whole, a very friendly lot. If you are a beginner and really fancy organising an event — no matter how small — make contact with an established rally organiser in your locality. He will be very happy to put you on the right lines. Rally organisation is an exacting and responsible job as the smallest mistake can have serious repercussions.

As with so many other aspects of rallying, the message is: pay attention to detail.

Motor sport can be dangerous and whether you are a driver, marshal or spectator, you are more likely to come across an accident than the average motorist, so it makes sense to know a little about first aid. The following points are not intended to be exhaustive — just a brief guide to what to do at an accident.

Protect the scene of the accident by sending someone up the road to slow or stop following cars. If you get hurt you won't be able to help anyone.

Switch off ignitions and stop people smoking — obvious, of course, but people with frayed nerves may light up.

Check the breathing of any casualties not able to speak. If someone is NOT breathing, tilt their head back, pinch their nose shut and blow air into their lungs — their chest should rise. Remove your mouth from the casualty's mouth, let air out; repeat every five seconds until breathing restarts. (This is mouth to mouth resuscitation and is one of the most important things to learn; try to see a practical demonstration sometime — it's not difficut.)

If someone is bleeding badly, press on the bleeding area firmly with your fingers, thumb and hand; if help is available, replace with dry dressing and a firm bandage. Ensure that bleeding stops — if not, revert to hand pressure.

Do not remove a casualty from a car unless there is real danger, eg fire or drowning, because they may have a fractured spine. Wait for skilled help.

Unconscious casualties outside a vehicle should be placed in the "$\frac{3}{4}$ prone position", ie almost face down. Ensure they are breathing easily — if not, apply mouth to mouth resuscitation; DO NOT LEAVE until they regain consciousness.

Send someone to get skilled help — ambulance, rescue vehicle, etc.

Remember that things which fall off a rally car may be very HOT. Kick broken exhausts out of the way, don't pick them up.

Try not to panic. It may not be easy but if you can keep calm while everyone else is flapping about, you may save someone's life.

11 The classic rallies

There are many good rallies for the young enthusiast to aim for during his career but only a few have that magical mixture of a tough route, good organisation, some tradition and, above all, that intangible ingredient X which makes them classics. In the authors' opinions, three stand above the rest:

1. *The Monte Carlo Rally*

The only event with more than one starting point, it is far and away the best known rally – in market research exercises it is often the *only* rally identified by the general public! Occasional organisational lapses over the years may have tarnished the legend slightly among competitors but it still gets very large entries, with a high proportion of private owners.

The rally is split into sections:

i)   A concentration run from several starting points to Monte Carlo. Towards the end of this there are five or six stages to establish a running order from then on (to avoid baulking).

No event offers more 'atmosphere' than the Monte Carlo Rally. Bruno Saby's Renault slithers past a well-patronised watering-hole.

ii) A common run from Monte back to Monte for the top 200 of around 1500km which includes fifteen special stages.

iii) The final night for the top hundred survivors. This is around 700km and includes ten special stages, some of which are done twice.

All the stages in the rally are on surfaced roads, closed to the public for the rally but all open for practising beforehand.

The final night of the Monte is possibly the most dramatic in rallying – keep an eye open in rally films for shots taken at the top of the classic Turini. Magic! Occasionally, hooligan spectators spread snow on unexpected corners which is less than entertaining.

Don't be put off by the works teams and their 600 tyres; beg, borrow or steal some old studded tyres, mortgage the house, sell the hi-fi and have a go at it; you will be able to dine out on it for months.

There are not so many Beautiful People about on the rally as at the Grand Prix but Monte in January can still be very pleasant.

2. The Lombard R.A.C. Rally

As your 'home' classic this is certainly one you should work towards in your development as a rally driver. Virtually 'forest racing' with no practising allowed. This causes some concern as many Europeans feel that British drivers have a distinct advantage in getting to know the forests through using them on other rallies – but this doesn't stop Scandinavians winning fairly regularly (which is perhaps why the rally is so popular with them).

Spectator interest has to be seen to be believed. In fact, the enthusiasm causes problems because stages sometimes have to be cancelled because of crowd congestion.

Despite a high entry fee (because of forestry charges) it is still a 'must' in your competition career. If you want to get noticed by the works teams, grit your teeth and try to lead the rally by the end of the first day. Better still, try to lead it by the end of the last day!

The Lombard-RAC Rally always offers a variety of weather. And when it snows, no one is happier than Hannu Mikkola.

A 'swinging Safari' for Finland's Ari Vatanen. He and Ulsterman Terry Harryman on their way to a win in 1983.

3. *The Safari*

Some of the mystery has filtered away now that several Europeans have won the Safari but it still remains a tremendous challenge against time and the elements. One of the few rallies not divided into 'stages'. It is one stage from start to finish – usually at an average of over 60mph! Then remember that it is either very, very wet or very, very muddy and you see why it is for men, not boys.

The Safari takes place entirely in Kenya (at Easter) and, because of the travel costs, is well nigh prohibitively expensive for European private owners. Mind you, if you can get there somehow you needn't be deterred by the calibre of the entry which falls off badly after the first dozen or so cars.

Be prepared for Safari fever – in other words, nerves – which sometimes puts even the most experienced drivers on edge. There is no known antidote.

The battles between teams over planes and helicopters are almost as entertaining as the rally – but don't blame them for laying on lavish service when every service point is practically a pit stop: if someone passes you while you are at a service point you may have to follow in their dust for miles.

Long may the Safari survive. It probably will – as long as it attracts world interest as it does at present (including extensive coverage on Japanese TV).

Incidentally, although this book isn't intended to be a travel guide, Kenya is worth a visit just for the wildlife.

So those are our three classics. A few others worth considering:

The 1000 Lakes Rally

This is the Finnish forest Grand Prix and has remained unchanged in character for quite some time. It is the fastest rally in the world series with average speeds of nearly 80mph. The winners have usually covered colossal practice miles, although pressure from residents on the rally route has led to strict limits on recce speeds being imposed – could this be a foretaste of what could happen throughout Europe?

If you think of Finns as wild men, be prepared for a shock when you see them on the road sections – they are meticulous in obeying speed limits because there are heavy rally penalties for breaking the law; the police have been known to put rally stickers on otherwise plain cars in order to catch people speeding!

You may see marks made on roads on the stages – these are where spectators have wagered who will 'yump' the furthest among their heroes. There are regularly 10,000 paying spectators on stages – very well controlled by marshals with Alsatian dogs.

The 1000 Lakes has never been won by a non-Scandinavian and only rarely by a non-Finn. That could be opportunity you hear knocking.

The Portugal Rally

This event has grown up over the last decade and features many classic stages. If you think the 1000 Lakes or RAC rallies are popular, the Portugal event will astound you – over $1\frac{1}{2}$ million spectators make some stages like driving through a tunnel!

Good prize money and 'assisted passages' are available for overseas entrants. Petrol is expensive though – and guard your property well.

Now you know why they're called 'Flying Finns'. This particular one is Ari Vatanen on the 1000 Lakes Rally – the fastest rally in the world.

German star Walter Röhrl entertains the usual huge crowds in Portugal.

Lady in a hurry! Michèle Mouton (who else?) on the Acropolis Rally.

The Acropolis

A great stage event over 2600km of rough roads and what look like goat tracks. 800 magnificent kilometres of special stages. A qualifying event for six national (as well as the world) championships and usually a big entry.

Very tough, very fast, very demanding but ... don't shy away. Greece is glorious at the time of year and it is an ideal rally to combine with a holiday: take your car down on a trailer because you stand a fair chance of breaking down.

Some others

Much less expensive than the above is the 24 Hours of Ypres Rally in Belgium. With two night runs, and easy to recce stages this is an ideal event for someone tackling a foreign rally for the first time.

Even nearer home, the Welsh and Scottish have a lot of attraction, both being excellent practice for the R.A.C. Rally. The Scottish is rough and you may get through a lot of tyres but it is a super event through glorious country and with a fine social side.

The Welsh is one of the cheapest of the home classics and a 'must' on your way to tackling the Lombard R.A.C.

The Manx also provides a cheap recce event with high speed tarmac stages where you can practise pace-notes.

If Easter in Ireland is your scene then the Circuit of Ireland will be high on your list. But don't be lulled by the social side — it is a tough, demanding rally. Tarmac stages on closed roads add to the joy. Limited practising allowed although obviously the classic stages get well known, being used year after year.

Some would argue that the Swedish Rally is better than the 1000 Lakes. Certainly it is different, being the only World Championship event held entirely on snow and ice. Regulations on studded tyres might mean you need special ones just for the one event. And it is a lot colder in Sweden in winter than in Finland in August!

Very expensive and a long way away but with a character all of its own is the Tour de Corse. Thousands and thousands of corners but, curiously, if you've done Welsh road rallies you won't feel totally at sea in Corsica. One of life's more enriching experiences!

Get out of that! British privateers Andrew Wood and Gordon Hood enjoying winter driving on the Swedish Rally.

The Tour de Corse is fast and furious.

Finally, keep an eye open for the "odd balls" — rallies run in weird and wonderful places for the strangest reasons. Show interest and present a good case and you could end up getting financial support from organisers who are working closely with tourist boards.

If you find the loot to tackle a programme of major events, you may get interested in one of the championships:

1. *World Rally Championship for Makes and Drivers*

Around a dozen qualifying events with ten points for first overall, down to one point for tenth, with a class scoring system on top. Minimum length of the qualifying events must be 2000km with at least 200km of tests. A very expensive series to do and few manufacturers tackle all rounds in this Championship seriously, which makes it difficult for rallying to have the same general public appeal as, say, Formula One, where all cars and drivers do all the qualifying rounds.

The series includes a World Rally Drivers Championship — because (hard though it may be for manufacturers to accept it) people are interested in people.

2. *European Rally Championship for Drivers*

Lots of qualifying events — generally shorter than the World Championship ones. Our advice if you feel like tackling it? Lie down until the feeling goes away. If you need further convincing, stop the next one hundred people you see and ask them who is the current European Rally Champion (or World Champion for that matter). No one will know.

12 Teams, and service crews

The team

Like much to do with rallying, *organisation* is the key to a successful rally team. All parts of the team must work efficiently. Nothing must be left to chance. When organising a rally team the most unexpected must always be expected; that may sound 'double Dutch' but a professional team will try to plan for every contingency *before* it actually happens. The Team manager of a professional team will make sure that his service cars carry the most obscure spare parts and everything will have been checked fully and nothing left to chance.

Even then, some things are totally unforeseeable. Many years ago Timo Makinen and Henry Liddon – one of the most professional crews ever to rally – made a call for snow tyres for a Scottish Rally. Yes, the sunny Scottish Rally! It was quite unthinkable that it would snow in Scotland in June and Dunlops thought Ford's Team Manager had taken leave of his senses when snow tyres were ordered. You've guessed – it snowed in the Highlands and covered several stages. Like many Finns, Makinen had a fixation about snow accoutrements and once had snow chains flown out to Kenya to see if they'd work in red murrum mud!

Here we give examples of some of the things that a professional team might organise when competing on a typical international event. On some rallies like the Safari or Monte Carlo there might be special problems needing a great deal of attention; on other events the problems might be simpler. For instance, there might be no tyre choices or no overseas travel to worry about – two of the most time-consuming topics.

If a team is competing on an overseas event all travel movements must be planned in detail. Boat and air tickets should be booked in good time and a travel itinerary be produced.

Plenty of time must be allowed for personnel to get to the start of a rally, particularly mechanics and service cars. Mechanics should be given time to check over cars before the start and drivers time to test them.

Most teams produce a booklet giving instructions to service crews, ranging from general notes about the positions of service boards and mobile radio to detailed rally car arrival times at service points. Instructions for drivers and navigators will also be included and will cover topics as varied as hotel reservations, emergency telephone numbers and even notes on known sections of route. A team 'Bible' can run to over 150 pages for a complicated international event.

A team should always hold a briefing meeting before the start at which details of each service point are discussed fully so that *everyone* is familiar with his own role on the event. A well-organised team will arrange tickets for post-rally functions and will even give advice on dress before and after the event. For instance, team ties, sweaters or blazers help to give a team a tidy, professional image and should be supplied to all personnel if budgets run to it.

Long before an event, an organised team will have numerous meetings where drivers and mechanics compare notes, discuss the rally and its mechanical requirements and make plans in detail. *107*

These planning meetings between team managers, drivers, navigators and mechanics always pay dividends.

Running a rally team is just like running any other sports team, be it professional or amateur. Everything must knit together and it is the responsibility of the Team Manager or his deputy to see that harmony abounds.

A good Team Manager will iron out any problems almost before they occur. It is surprising how petty some of the top drivers, co-drivers and mechanics can be. Despite the large fees that some team personnel may be earning, there can only be one boss and that is the Team Manager. He must stamp on any squabbles!

If you are running your own small team — maybe made up of club members — it will be a little more difficult to play the heavy hand as a Team Manager for, after all, the team members may be paying for everything out of their own pockets. Nevertheless, without being dictatorial, the person whose job it is to handle the team should try to follow the guidelines set by the professionals. The main thing is to keep every one informed at all times. Let there be no secrets.

Service crews

Throughout this book we have referred to service crews and their importance cannot be underestimated. Although their presence is not strictly necessary and is probably even *unwelcome,* and may be forbidden, on road rallies, there is no doubt that service crews are a necessary part of stage rallying. As speeds of rally cars increase, as stages become rougher and as rallies become longer the more important become the service crews.

There may be a vast difference between the professional works service crew and the amateur, but by describing some of the methods of the former, we hope that amateurs might benefit. To works service crews the rally is a job of work for which they are paid and whilst they are totally dedicated to their job and to the sport, they cannot be expected to do anything 'purely for love of it'. In other words, they will be reimbursed at the appropriate rate for the job and should be provided with first class equipment.

A good service crew will consist of two or three mechanics in an estate car or van. They will all be skilled and capable of all types of mechanical work, although one or other may have special knowledge of some particular subject, for example: electrics or engines. They will have every conceivable spare part on board although obviously nothing unnecessary will be carried as the weight of the service vehicle is important.

The service crew will be prepared to go anywhere providing arrangements are made for them, and whilst they will have no illusions about their driving abilities they will all be competent drivers in all weather conditions. At least one member of the crew will be equally competent at map reading, and will have the ability to plot references, interpret time schedules and generally keep the service car on the right route.

A good rally mechanic will enjoy the challenge of his work and will cheerfully work in the most outrageous conditions if the success of the team depends upon it. Works mechanics are frequently seen working in sub-zero temperatures or in mud and rain.

	FORD MOTOR CO. LTD.								
SERVICE SCHEDULE	COMPETITIONS DEPARTMENT			..........R A C INTERNATIONAL...RALLY					
CREW NO. 5	NAMES	J RUSHBROOK/P CHOPPING	DATE	SUN/MON. 23/24 NOV.		COMPETITION NUMBERS	1, 6, 14		

SPECIAL INSTRUCTIONS:-

NO.	PLACE	MAP	REF.	ARRIVE BY	FIRST CAR DUE	DISTANCE	TRAVELLING TIME	AVERAGE	COMPETITORS COMING FROM	REMARKS/ROUTE
22	After SS 19 CIRENCESTER PARK In Service Area	163	989 018	12.00	12.35	206m.	–	–	–	With Crew 1. Approach on A419. Enter Park at Spot Height 126.
29	Before and after SS 25 Yellow crossroads Near Round House.	181	985 356	20.15	20.45	88m.	6h 45m.	6mph.	S	Off Route. Go through Severn Bridge Service Area for new tyres from Dunlop.
36	After SS 35 Yellow road 1½m. from ST HARMON	136	016 719	03.58	04.27	145m.	6hrs.	24mph.	E	Off Route.
42	After SS 42 TC 13 BETWS-Y-COED	115	797 559	11.25	11.55	76m.	5h 35m.	13mph.	–	With Dunlop and Crews 2 and 6. Replenish tyres from Dunlop.
47	YORK RACECOURSE Service Area	105	600 497	17.45	18.16	161m.	4h 15m.	37mph. (incl. Motorway)	–	With all other Crews and Dunlop. Full Check Each Car.

A page from a works team Service schedule. Average speeds are kept very low and precise locations of service points are given. A service crew must be able to plot map references and read a map.

Service vehicles come in all shapes ...

... and sizes!

The 'Cafe' sign might suggest a more exotic location – but this is, in fact, the Talbot team servicing on the Lombard-RAC Rally in Yorkshire!

A typical road-side service point on a British international rally. Service crews should make sure they have due regard for the countryside and leave the area as they found it.

ROUTE FOR SERVICE VEHICLES

Note that penalties may be applied to any competitor whose Service Crew is found to be contravening the regulations.

North Wales Police have informed us that RADAR speed checks may be made during the event.

START	L.S.P. MOTORS, LLANDUDNO.	115/790½820½
	via A546 to	
SERVICE AREA 'A'	WEST SHORE CAR PARK, LLANDUDNO.	115/773½816
	via A546, A55, A470 to	
SERVICE AREA 'B'	CAE LLAN CAR PARK, BETWS-Y-COED.	115/795 565
	via A5, A4086, A498 to	
SERVICE AREA 'C'	PUBLIC CAR PARK, BEDDGELERT.	115/589 481
	via A4085, A487, A470 to	
SERVICE AREA 'D'	FARMERS' MART, DOLGELLAU.	124/729 180½
	via A494 to	
SERVICE AREA 'E'	GREEN CAR PARK, BALA.	125/929 361
	via A4212, B4501, A5, A470 to	
SERVICE AREA 'F'	MEADOW VALE GARAGE, LLANRWST. (Park in old road loop)	116/806 605½

Service vehicles can cause more trouble than rally cars, so very often the organisers will give details of service areas and the routes to be taken. These instructions were issued on the Gwynedd Rally.

A service point in Monte Carlo.

It's all hands on deck when time is short. Note the teamwork of the Opel mechanics , whilst Ford's crack mechanic Mick Jones displays his more handsome features to the camera on a Monte Carlo Rally!

But too many cooks could spoil the broth!

Hannu Mikkola's Audi Quattro receives some emergency service. Notice how the crew waits patiently and does not interfere!

To see any real expert doing his job to the best of his ability is a joy, and to see a rally mechanic working with precision at high speed under difficult conditions is as exciting as watching a star driver in full cry: crowds at service points endorse this. Like all professionals, they will take certain precautions and may alter brackets and mounting points to facilitate removal and replacement of parts when valuable seconds count. (Taking care not to break homologation rules, of course.) They even make special tools which can get into awkward spots and so save further vital seconds.

Many people think that the life of an international works rally mechanic is one of glamorous jet-setting and mingling with the famous. True, these things do come into the mechanic's life but 90% of his life is pure, solid, honest-to-goodness hard work. He probably enjoys travelling and seeing new places but it is remarkable how quickly mechanics become accustomed to the glamorous surroundings to which their work takes them. Some might think that they are *blasé* to the extreme, but this would be an unfair interpretation. It won't be uncommon to hear two rally mechanics sitting beneath the tailgate of their service car in a remote African village discussing the latest doings of Manchester United or Nottingham Forest, oblivious of their exotic location!

Service crews must be equipped with the right clothing, whatever climate they are working in. They should always carry at least two pairs of overalls each (one for working in dirty conditions and the other for use at scrutineering and other times when they are not expecting to become covered with mud). They should have good strong boots (some prefer sporting shoes for greater agility), warm underwear and extra sets of waterproof gear. A warm, fur-lined 'Parka' is a good thing to have as well. Don't expect a service mechanic to wear a rally jacket for work and manage to keep it clean – he'll have to be equipped with more than one rally jacket. As we have said elsewhere, oily rally jackets in hotel bars do not present a good team image.

Preparation of the service car or van is almost as important as the preparation of the rally car. First and foremost, it is wise to build a solid grille between the driver's compartment and the rear area, as numerous accidents have happened as a *113* result of jacks, welding bottles or halfshafts flying about inside the car. Furthermore, everything which is heavy should be strapped down. A roof rack is necessary to carry extra wheels and bigger items such as a propshaft or welding bottle. Inside the car there should be plenty of small drawers for every conceivable size of nut, bolt and washer. Every drawer and compartment should be labelled and things stored in a logical way.

There should be plenty of light inside the rear of the service car and several spare torches as well as a powerful inspection light which should have a lead long enough to reach right round the car.

When a works service crew arrives at its predetermined spot (well ahead of its first potential customer) it will park off the public highway, on level ground if possible. It is common for numerous service cars to cluster together in lay-bys or service areas, so it is important for crews to have a good, luminous or even illuminated service board. A simple luminous board is ideal, and should carry the team badge or some simple message or code: long-winded messages are not necessary. A private team's service crew once inadvertently left their service board behind after leaving a service point in a Welsh village. The board was, in fact, a modified racing pit signal kit with removable letters. It was

with some chagrin that they discovered, on a return visit to the village, their beloved sign outside a tea shop with the letters re-arranged to advertise cream teas!

Most service crews favour lights on long poles as a method of identifying their location. Hopefully, these can be seen above the rest of the rabble but in reality there are often so many tall poles carrying flashing lights that the view for the approaching rally crews is like that of pilots approaching Heathrow Airport!

All professional teams use radios and these can be a boon to a service crew on any size of event. Ensure that the radios are legal, licensed, tuned to the right wavelength and that the organisers have not banned their use for any reason.

A service crew should keep the radio 'live' at all times in case there's an emergency call for assistance from their rally car. You'd be surprised how many times rally cars have minor mechanical 'panics' and scream for assistance. Very often on an event like the Lombard R.A.C., the Acropolis or the San Remo, an 'off-duty' service crew driving to their next service point will pick up the call and give help. They must be careful not to be late at their next service point, of course, thereby jeopardising the entire team.

CREW No.	Sv. Pt.	Road Book / Map Ref.	Location	Aft SS	At TC	Arrv By	1st Car due	Routing	Dist	Serv Time	Dir App	P	Tyres	Special Comments
														CODASUR RALLY SERVICE SCHEDULE SHEET 5 — CAR NO'S 3 + 10
SUP + 3	30	1/4 0.00+	PARC FERMÉ EXIT TUCUMAN	—	31	0645 THURS	0700	SEE TOWN PLAN	—	5	—	FULL 1bg	—	SUP. LEAVE TUC. IMMED. 3 — " — 0830 LATEST.
1	31	9/4 101.63	R308 J.B. ALBERDI AT YPF STATION	BEF 14	—	0930 TH.	0810	R.38 J.B. ALBERDI R308 TO S.P.	150k (50k/h)	15	N + E	12g	AS SP28	LEAVE TUCUMAN 0530 LATEST — " — LEAVE SP 11.00 LATEST
2	32	17/4 82.92	R308/R10 15 km North of LA MERCED	AFT 14	—	0900	0930	R38 LA MERCED R10/R308 TO S.P.	200k (50k/h)	5	W + N	ABS FULL 1bg	ARI:175 B 225 B DOM: PN175B 195B	LEAVE TUCUMAN 0500 LATEST. — " — LEAVE SP 1100 LATEST
4 + SUP.	33	30/4 118.27+	R11 EL VALLECITO IMMED. AFTER SS FINISH	AFT 15	—	1100	1130	R301 S. PEDRO & FRIAS R11 EL VALLECITO	4: 250k (50k/h) SUP. (60k/h)	15	NN	FULL 1bg	ARI: 175B 225B DOM: PN175B 195B	LEAVE TUCUMAN 0600 LATEST — " — SUP. LEAVE SP 1200 LATEST.
3 + SUP	34	41/4 101.42	R156/R64 X-RDS LAVALLE AFTER RLWY-X	AFT 16	—	1230	1315	R301 S. PEDRO LAVALLE	3: 200 (50k/L) SUP. 150k (60k/L)	15	W	15g	ARI: 175-14 225-B DOM: PN175B 195B	SUP. LEAVE 13.30 LATEST.
1	35	48/4 86.70	BEFORE TC 36 RIO DULCE TERMAS DE RIO HONDO	AFT 17	BEF 36	1400	1450	R333 GRANEROS R301 CHOCIGASTA WC TO R9 AND TERMAS.	150k (60 k/h)	5	S	10g	NO CHANGE	COMMENCE FINAL CHECKS.
2 + SUP.	36	51/4 82.41	SHELL STN R9 JUST OUTSIDE TUCUMAN	—	BEF 37	1500	1550	R38 TUCUMAN AND BACK OUT ON R9	2: 200k (50k/h) SUP: 150k (60k/h)	20	S	4g	NO CHANGE	COMPLETE FINAL CHECKS. SUP. TO FOLLOW TO PARC FERME AND COLLECT CREW.
SUP.	37	54/4 4.61	PARC FERMÉ ENTRANCE TUCUMAN	—	—	ASAP	1617	R157, R301 TUCUMAN ETC.	—	—	—	—	—	RETURN ALL WHEELS + TYRES TO PIRELLI. ALL PARTS TO PARAGUAY TRUCK ALL STAY HOTEL VIENA TUCUMAN.

This is the page from the Rothmans team's service schedule on Argentina's 'Codasur' Rally. This rally presented major problems for service crews as vast distances were involved between most points.

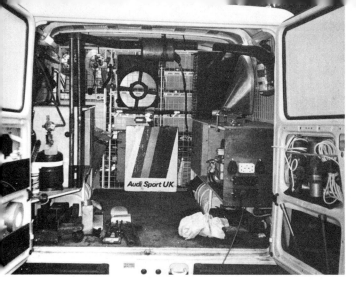

Service vehicles should be neatly and sensibly packed.

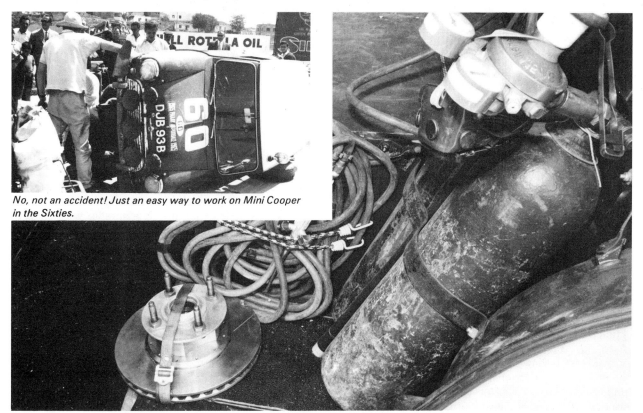

No, not an accident! Just an easy way to work on Mini Cooper in the Sixties.

Heavy items in a service car MUST be well strapped down to stop them flying into mechanics in an accident.

On normal occasions, the co-driver will radio forward to a service crew and advise them of the car's approximate time of arrival, the jobs that need to be done and the amount of time available. The good mechanic will then lay out the appropriate tools, not unlike a surgeon preparing for an operation.

When organising service, always try to avoid breaking the rules. Service areas – or, more importantly, forbidden service areas – will be shown by the organisers. They are given for a reason, so obey them.

Most teams resort to unmarked supervision cars and there is now a tendency to employ 'chase' cars which virtually cover the rally route. When vital World Championship points are at stake, teams have been known to enter cars purely as support vehicles, the 'navigators' of these cars being mechanics. Where will it all end? Mind you, racing and rally cars used to carry 'riding mechanics' fifty years ago. Maybe we've come full circle!

A frequent question posed to team managers and mechanics is: 'What makes a good rally mechanic?'. Basically the mechanic should be technically capable, have deep interest in rallying and be able to work quickly in difficult conditions. He will like to see his driver succeed in an event and will be unflappable under the most difficult conditions.

13 Sponsorship

Sponsorship came to the rally scene in the late Sixties and although opinions differ about the good or bad effect it has had on the sport, there is no doubt that it has changed it. The extra promotional efforts of the sponsors have helped to establish rallying as a major sport, although there's still a long way to go in this direction – how many rally drivers are household names like their counterparts from football, cricket, snooker, golf or showjumping? None, and sheepdog trials and fishing still gain more British television exposure than rallying.

Nevertheless, in the Eighties the whole sponsorship business has become more professional and major sponsors have been attracted to rallying regarding it, quite rightly, as a sport still in its commercial infancy.

So, let us look at the opportunities for sponsorship.

For a start, there are four basic areas on which potential sponsors can set their sights: sponsorship of an individual car, a team of cars, an actual event or a full rally championship. Other more peripheral areas are the sponsorship of individual drivers or single stages on rallies. As with any other sport, the opportunities are endless – although whether they all make sound commercial sense is another matter and we'll come to that later.

Levels of sponsorship vary tremendously, from free meat from the local butcher in exchange for his name on the side of a club rally car to the £1 million or more demanded by manufacturers to contest a full World Championship season in a sponsor's colours. And remember, a most important factor to bear in mind is that the actual negotiated fee is only half the story: to gain full benefit from sponsorship one has to equal the amount of cash laid out initially with expenditure on 'follow-up' promotion, advertising and P.R.

Dealing at club level first, practically every car on all but the smallest twelve car event seems to attract some form of sponsorship. Probably fifty per cent of this sponsorship money is wasted but very often such a sponsor will turn out to be an altruistic uncle who doesn't really see rallying as the main marketing weapon for his brand of cream cakes or canned prunes but genuinely likes to support his nephew and also get a bit of fun out of life. And why not?

The position of the British Inland Revenue on these and all other sponsorship ventures is not quite so magnanimous. According to them, sponsorship expenses will generally not be allowed against tax unless the reason for the sponsorship was "wholly and exclusively for the purposes of the company's trade". You have been warned!

In the case of a private entry sponsored for an event or series of events, it is most important to have the car and crew (and support vehicles, if any) well presented. Providing the fee is sufficient to cover costs, the car should be sprayed and lettered in accordance with the sponsor's liveries and trading styles. A major advertiser working in collaboration with a major team will probably take the initiative but a company that is not so familiar with sponsorship may need some help from the rally crew. A plan should be made and photographs, press releases and other forms of promotional material prepared.

Many people abuse sponsorship; it is simply not enough to take a sponsor's fee, plonk his name on your car and rally jacket, then leave it at that. Be prepared to appear with the car at fêtes or other social functions if the sponsor is likely to benefit – many open-air functions each summer will welcome a rally car or two for display.

A sponsor should be given due credit at any function (though don't plug him so blatantly that people are actually put off) and the sponsor's money should be used wisely. If a sponsor has a particular local area for his business activity, then it is unwise for the crew to concentrate on events at the other end of the country.

The R.A.C.M.S.A. impose restrictions on spon-

Small private teams should be well turned out – just like professionals. This type of photograph could be useful publicity for local sponsors.

sorship and it is important that people hunting for support be fully aware of the details. Different licence grades allow different levels of advertising on cars. Basically a driver/entrant's licence allows you to have the name of the entrant, driver and make of car in lettering approximately four inches high on each side of the car, plus a maximum of five decals on each side, each no bigger than the size of a shoe box lid.

Any further advertising requires an advertising permit from the R.A.C.M.S.A. This permit allows unlimited advertising subject to certain provisos and is available in three grades – Restricted (£40), National (£80) and International (£170). With these licences you can paint almost anything you like on the car provided it isn't obscene of course. Also, you will have to fork out another £35 for an entrant's licence if you want your sponsor's name in the rally programme.

The beginner must recognise that it is extremely difficult to obtain worthwhile sponsorship. Most commercial organisations receive approaches

of some sort every day – either from worthwhile charities or sports offering guaranteed TV exposure. Consider for a moment – a company could probably sponsor a televised basketball or other sports game for *less* than the cost of backing one rally car in a serious programme. Which would you choose on straight commercial grounds? No wonder even the works teams often find it difficult to obtain sponsors. A lot of people think that a works Team Manager merely picks up the 'phone and nets the first large advertiser he contacts – this simply is not so.

Some people produce a leaflet or brochure showing details of their past successes, details of the crew and an outline of what the combination and proposed programme can offer a prospective sponsor. If you do this, try to be original and have the thing professionally designed. One thing many people forget is to give an indication of the amount of money involved – they foolishly expect the prospective sponsor to suggest a figure.

Russell Brookes and his 'Andrews Heat for *117*

Hire' sponsorship has been something of a copy-book example that many others might wish to emulate. In the mid Seventies, Brookes was hoping to attract a sponsor as he was confident in his own driving ability having achieved successes in Ford Mexico Championship events. He and his navigator John Brown put together a professional brochure listing the benefits of sponsorship and explaining the sport and its following. Brookes managed to interest a young, growing company by the name of Andrews and they offered limited support 'to see how things went'. As we now know, the Andrews business grew and so did Russell's sponsorship budget and he put a lot of effort into keeping Andrews informed and worked hard to give his sponsor real value. Many drivers fall down in this respect. Mind, not all sponsors make all they should out of the sport.

MORECAMBE CAR CLUB LTD.

PRESENTS THE

illuminations

THE FIRST ROUND OF THE

Motoring *News* *1983*

RALLY CHAMPIONSHIP

19th/20th FEBRUARY 1983

sponsored by

MIDAC RACING

of Morecambe

Supplementary Regulations

Make sure the sponsors are given good exposure on the rally regulations and all other printed matter. Here are examples from club and international categories.

REGLEMENT—REGULATIONS

Rallying has been a major weapon in the advertising plans of 'Andrews Heat for Hire'. This is Russell Brookes' Vauxhall Chevette.

120 A good sponsor to have for an expensive sport!

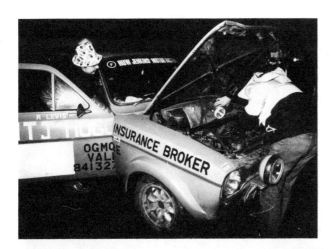

Sponsorship can come from all sorts of unlikely sources ...

121

A club rally start may lack some of the glamour and razzamataz of an international — but none of the enthusiasm. These photographs show two levels of event sponsorship.

Rothmans have used rallying well as a major promotional weapon, probably the first 'non motoring product' to use our sport as a marketing platform. They have involved themselves successfully in sponsorship of drivers, teams, events and championships, not only in Britain but in several other major overseas markets. Despite Rothmans' successes (their drivers Ari Vatanen and David Richards won the World Championship in 1981 then Walter Röhrl and Christian Geistdorfer repeated the feat for them the year after) they never forgot the roots of the sport and spent a good proportion of their budget attempting to reach the club enthusiast through film shows, club literature, rally equipment, clothing etc. They advertised heavily to the rally enthusiast but also took it a stage further and actually took rallying into the High Street with a series of 48-sheet posters and expensive national advertising prior to the Lombard R.A.C. Rally. For Rothmans, and all other sponsors of their size, each area of expenditure has to be dealt with separately, then locked in to a complex overall plan.

On a lesser scale, most organisers of events who have managed to obtain sponsorship would do well to have an early discussion with their sponsors to establish their aims, their markets and any direct results they are hoping to achieve as a result of the collaboration. For instance, in the case of a local stage rally, a sponsor whose marketing area is within the confines of the start and finish points of a rally might well feel his expenditure justified by the local press coverage. Others might want more, so if you are seeking sponsorship for an event (often very necessary to offset high organisational costs) put yourself in the potential sponsor's shoes. Ask: what will he get out of it? Then ask yourself: would I spend the same money in such a way?

To sponsor a World Championship Rally will probably cost an advertiser in excess of £75,000. A local stage rally might cost a sponsor only £200 but both situations have a great deal in common and the deciding factor at the end of the day returns to sound common sense and plain value for money.

If the sponsorship fee warrants it, an organising club may offer to incorporate the sponsor's name in a rally title and thereby guarantee the sponsor's being mentioned in any media reports. A classic example of this is Britain's major event, the much-loved R.A.C. Rally which is now referred to as the "Lombard — R.A.C." thanks to the long-term links between sponsor and organiser.

One thing to remember, though. Do not offer to alter the name of an event purely for one year, then change sponsors and therefore the name of the rally the next year. Continuity is necessary from everyone's point of view and a rally can quickly lose its reputation if it never has the same name twice.

Readers of this book will probably be more interested in sponsorship for individual cars and teams rather than events and championships. The only constant factor is the hard work which is necessary to obtain sponsorship then make it effective. A sponsor will not get maximum value from his involvement by merely sticking his name on a car or by tagging it to an event; the sponsor and the sponsored must work hard to obtain every ounce of benefit.

Let us end this chapter with a question: what makes you think *you* deserve sponsorship? Rallying doesn't owe you a living and unless you have won something – and something worthwhile – don't expect people to rush to give you money so that you can continue what is after all your sport and hobby.

Finally let us repeat that if you achieve a few wins and as a result get sponsorship then don't just take the money and run. Work at the deal and give the sponsor value. That way you stand a chance of keeping them for another year.

14 Crystal gazing...

Hopefully, this book will have encouraged you to take up rallying. If it has, you may wonder just what sort of future the sport has in store. Well, we can't see into our crystal ball for all the sponsors' stickers on it but really we need to look at the future in three steps: short, medium and long term.

In the short term the most immediate task is for the sport to fight harder for itself in the U.K. to get a proper share of facilities and access to stages. As people have more leisure, sport inevitably will have to be better coordinated – which means committees. Which means that the sport must have proper representation on these committees. If not, we will be frozen out by bikers and hikers, as well as all sorts of other sports. The R.A.C.M.S.A. will have to appoint someone whose sole job it is to walk the corridors of power to see that the right representations are made to the right authorities at the right time.

Rallying is not a sport we need to be ashamed of; it is a sport which gives a lot of pleasure to a lot of people, either as competitors, officials or spectators: we should argue our case for facilities with vigour.

Sadly at the moment we don't help ourselves very much. Many motor clubs are far too parochial in their approach. There are too many clubs hovering around the 80 or so membership figure and there is far too little liaison between clubs. Clubs need to promote themselves and the sport better. How many clubs take an active part in their local community affairs so that they are seen to be responsible people, not just rock apes with noisy, smelly cars? Precious few. How many clubs work with local charities so that they get good media coverage in their area? Again precious few.

What has all this hectoring got to do with you, we hear you cry? After all, you probably bought the book as something of a beginner. Well, simply this – those of us who have been in the sport for some time haven't made too good a job of sorting things out. If you come in with a new and fresh approach, you may be able to help safeguard the future of rallying.

Stepping gracefully down from the pulpit, let us consider one or two other short term aspects. Homologation needs sorting out; the hints and innuendoes about cheating just don't help our sport.

Costs must be kept down. If someone of eighteen wants to be a footballer he need spend little or nothing on equipment; he or she *could* be a tennis star at very little cost. If he wants to be the next Hannu Mikkola, somehow or other he has got to get behind the wheel of a car. The more we can do to make it easier for him the better. Let's see more 'one make' formulae, with the rules tightly written to keep expenses to a minimum. It goes without saying that anyone caught cheating should be slung out for a year.

Touch wood, but the spectator control problem, although serious, seems no worse than it was a year or two ago. However, the speeds of the cars keep going up so we would like to see the introduction of some form of power-to-experience formula. It could perhaps be done via a restrictor plate but somehow we must make it impossible for an absolute beginner to enter a rally in a full-house works replica. No one would expect to leap into Formula One without experience. Why should they do so in rallying? One, or two simple power-to-experience formulae would give rallying the e-quivalent of the Formula Ford, F3, F2 stepping stones into F1.

We remain reasonably optimistic about road rallying (which is still the best training ground for the disciplines of co-driving). If it ruthlessly disciplines itself, road rallying can have a future. Ruthless discipline means no cut-throat competitions and probably no championships. And the cars *must* be kept quiet. Maybe there should be a 1300cc limit?

In the medium term, much depends on the

Common Market. Yes, really, because inevitably any legislation passed on the motor vehicle is going to affect rallying.

Private tuners are going to find it increasingly difficult to get through legislation, which will leave manufacturers with a stranglehold on what is or isn't allowed.

We shall see an increasing shift to single stage events at the club level and there will still be letters in the enthusiast press calling for roads to be closed for rallying. We are not optimistic.

One thing rallying has to face in the medium and short term: much tougher competition from other sports. In the relatively brief period between the first and second editions of this book, darts and snooker are just two of the many sports which have increased in prominence and therefore attracted sponsors and spectators who might otherwise have turned to our beloved sport. This could be one reason why many clubs now face a shortage of marshals. And we shouldn't get carried away by the present volume of cigarette sponsorship for rallying. If this is banned — or the fag people turn to other sports for their own reasons — then the whole sponsorship scene could collapse.

Long term? Your crystal ball is as good as ours; it all depends on energy resources. Much as we all love rallying and much as we all shout about its benefits, we have to face facts. And the facts are that if people are shivering under blankets because they have no oil for central heating, then there is no way we will be rallying. We'd be lynched if we tried.

It won't come to that. Man's love affair with mobility via the motor car is a deep and lasting one. Man's ingenuity and drive will therefore lead him to overcome any energy problems we may see looming in the distance. And if we still have transport, a select band will still want to go faster to test themselves (there is no sign that the human race is losing its healthy desire for excitement).

If man still wants to go fast, then there will still be races and rallies. Come to think of it the way some roads are being maintained at the moment, rallying will be more challenging because the roads will be rougher!

We make no attempt to forecast what means man will use to continue motoring. It is difficult to see Tony Lanfranchi in 2001 (of course he will still be racing) going round Paddock Bend with a sail sticking up out of his car, and if we ever have electric cars then we will need a whole new breed of noise marshals — people to check that cars register at least a certain minimum noise level — if they don't the cars will be so quiet that spectators won't hear them coming, which will be dangerous!

To study the future, it is helpful to study the past. If you look back twenty years or so, rallying wasn't all that different then. You could find your way around quieter areas of the country today with the maps in use then and techniques with pace notes, servicing and so on have not advanced much since the early Sixties; some of the stars of the Sixties are still rallying, and rallying successfully (which is why there are such golden opportunities for a young person like you — they must retire sometime).

Overall we remain optimistic. Rallying will stay healthy at least until the turn of the century. Have fun!